For Every Urb

- Looking for a p
- Gridlock
- Unfriendly salesclerks
- Beepers and cell phones
- Smokers
- Nonsmokers
- Overcrowded subways and buses
- ATM panhandlers
- Pollution
- Long lines and slow service
- Broken pay phones
- Still looking for a parking space

There's *Urban Ease.*

DR. ALLEN ELKIN is a clinical psychologist, a certified sex therapist, and the director of the Stress Management & Counseling Center in New York City. Nationally known for his expertise in the field of stress and emotional disorders, he has appeared on *Today* and *Good Morning America,* as well as programs on PBS, CNN, FNN, and Fox 5. In addition, Dr. Elkin holds workshops for professional associations and corporations including the American Society of Contemporary Medicine and Surgery, the Drug Enforcement Agency, Morgan Stanley, IBM, PepsiCo, and the New York Stock Exchange. He lives in New York City with his wife and two children.

Urban Ease

Stress-free Living in the Big City

Allen Elkin, Ph.D.

A PLUME BOOK

PLUME
Published by the Penguin Group
Penguin Putnam Inc., 375 Hudson Street, New York, New York 10014, U.S.A.
Penguin Books Ltd, 27 Wrights Lane, London W8 5TZ, England
Penguin Books Australia Ltd, Ringwood, Victoria, Australia
Penguin Books Canada Ltd, 10 Alcorn Avenue, Toronto, Ontario, Canada M4V 3B2
Penguin Books (N.Z.) Ltd, 182–190 Wairau Road, Auckland 10, New Zealand

Penguin Books Ltd, Registered Offices: Harmondsworth, Middlesex, England

First published by Plume, a member of Penguin Putnam Inc.

First Printing, February, 1999
10 9 8 7 6 5 4 3 2 1

 REGISTERED TRADEMARK—MARCA REGISTRADA

LIBRARY OF CONGRESS CATALOGING-IN-PUBLICATION DATA:

Elkin, Allen.
    Urban ease : stress-free living in the big city / Allen Elkin.
        p.   cm.
    ISBN 0-452-27741-8
    1. City and town life—Psychological aspects.   2. Environmental
psychology.   3. Stress (Psychology)   4. Stress management.
I. Title.
BF353.5.C53E45   1999
155.9′042′091732—dc21   98-34778
                                                    CIP

Printed in the United States of America
Set in New Aster
Designed by Stanley S. Drate / Folio Graphics Co. Inc.

BOOKS ARE AVAILABLE AT QUANTITY DISCOUNTS WHEN USED TO PROMOTE PRODUCTS OR SERVICES. FOR
INFORMATION PLEASE WRITE TO PREMIUM MARKETING DIVISION, PENGUIN PUTNAM, INC., 375 HUDSON
STREET, NEW YORK, NEW YORK 10014.

For my wife, Beth, and our children, Josh and Katy.

Contents

PART TWO
Stress Relief Strategies

Introduction

I have been a city dweller for most of my life, but not always. Many happy years were spent living in a small Canadian town. I remember vividly the shock of moving to a much larger, American city and the dismay I felt having to compete with a dozen people for a single seat, or at least a place to stand, on the subway. I nostalgically recall the pleasant bicycle ride to my small-town office and remember that I rarely suffered through traffic and never double-locked my front door or got into a heated argument with a taxi driver.

Now my days are far less tranquil. The city guarantees that. It's always in your face, taunting you and testing you. Days without crisis are rare, and days without hassle are even harder to come by. And just when you think you've seen it all, the city finds a way to surprise you.

Still, I like big cities. Admittedly, my entire disposition would suggest otherwise; my temperament repeatedly clashes with the demands of urban life. On personality tests, I always choose (a), preferring to spend "A quiet evening at home," rather than (b) A wild night on the town, or even (c) Any kind of night on the town. Most everything about me suggests country, or at least small-town. Cities are high maintenance, and I am generally low maintenance. I need little stimulation. I like peace and quiet. I prefer a lifestyle without stress.

Yet as I write these words I am happily sitting in a neighborhood coffee shop about a block and a half from my house in the city. My table overlooks the street, which at this time of the day is overrun with people going about their Saturday chores. The street exudes vitality and excitement. I like being a few short blocks away from a favorite bakery, a good bookstore, a food market, and dozens of restaurants and cafes. I treasure the sense of community I feel when I'm in my neighborhood. I welcome a familiar face, yet delight in the anonymity that only a big city can provide. I enjoy exploring and discovering other parts of the city. I value the diversity of people and the babel of language. I like the options. I love the energy.

Indeed, on good days one can easily rave about the joys of city life. But there can be as many days when there's much *not* to feel charmed with. The fact is, most city dwellers relate to the city with this kind of ambivalence. Some people stay only because they have to—jobs, family commitments, or financial constraints make it necessary to remain there. For them, *leaving* the city would be the easiest way to de-stress their lives. They, like many others, consider the phrase "urban ease" to be an oxymoron.

Unfortunately, big cities do not come with instruction booklets or user manuals. No one has shown us how to cope with the stress and pressures of city life. No one has told us how to avoid the daily irritations and frustrations that come with urban living. At least until now.

This book provides you with a comprehensive approach to managing and minimizing your urban stress, showing you what you can do to extract satisfaction and joy from each day you live in the city. You will learn how you can avoid stress by looking at the city differently and reacting differently to the annoyances it presents. You can measure your current stress level and assess where it comes from and how it manifests itself. You can determine your "Hassle Quotient" (HQ), a measure of your stress-resilience.

The book also gives you the practical direction you need to start coping with specific problems, issues, and demands that punctuate your daily life. It shows you, step by step, how to eliminate or certainly reduce your levels of urban stress and manage the hassles of city living.

In this guide I have tried to be realistic. I recognize that your life is already complicated and demanding. I do not suggest that you sell your car, disconnect your telephone, or get up two hours earlier. I also recognize that you may not have lots of money. I do not tell you to hire a chauffeur, buy a fabulous weekend house in the country, or pay others to do all the things you hate. (Actually I *do* suggest some changes along these lines, but quite sensibly.)

When I talk of cities, I'm referring to our larger cities. Unlike their smaller cousins, big cities generate their own special kind of stress. Of course big cities themselves can differ one from another. The thought of lumping Los Angeles, Cleveland, Paris, Tokyo, Rochester, Mexico City, Dallas, San Francisco, Miami, and Bangkok into the same category boggles the mind. Some cities are dense, vertical, and congested, while others sprawl endlessly with few people per block. There are cities made for walking and there are cities made for driving. Yet, while every city is unique, they all share a common trait: They can be incredibly stressful.

Fortunately, you can learn how to avoid much if not most of this stress and minimize the strain of city life. You do not have to move to a cabin in rural Vermont, take up farming in Iowa, or retreat to the quieter parts of the Pacific Northwest. Thankfully, you can stay put. You can find more than enough contentment right here. You can learn to live your life with urban ease.

PART ONE

Urban Basics

1

City Woes

What gets me about the city are the crowds. Everywhere you go there are hordes of people. Everything is such a hassle. I hate the pushing, the shoving, and the rudeness. Why is it so hard for people to say, 'please,' 'thank you,' or 'excuse me,' once in a while?

It's the noise, the dirt, and the crime. And the crazies. I never know what stunt the guy next to me is going to pull. Frankly, it scares the hell out of me.

It takes a lot of money to live here. And I live in a shoe box. A very expensive shoe box.

*N*ot too long ago my wife, Beth, and I were having dinner with some friends and, as often happens, the topic of conversation turned to life in the city. Our friends had some news: They were moving. They were fed up with the crowds, the noise, the filth, the danger, their cramped apartment, the high rent . . . their list went on. For them, living in the city meant too much hassle and too much stress. They wanted out.

They are not alone. As a clinical psychologist specializing in stress management, I hear similar complaints in the workshops and seminars I conduct in many different parts of the country. It seems as if a growing number of city dwellers are unhappy about the quality of their lives and are blaming the city. These days more and more people are asking themselves: "Do I really want to live here?" Increasingly, many are asking a second question: "When can I leave?" Even Beth, usually a model of emotional equanimity, has on more than one occasion sighed audibly, smiled quizzically, and asked, "Tell me again. Why do we just *love* living here?"

While life anywhere has its share of annoyances and frustrations, big-city life can be even more aggravating. Whenever you have so many people living, working, shopping, and amusing themselves in such a relatively small space, there is bound to be friction, tension, and exasperation. Stress and big cities have always been synonymous and continue to be even more so.

Why, then, would anyone choose to live in such a stressful environment?

"A Nice Place to Visit, But . . ."

I have always been fascinated by books or articles that show us how to pick the "best" places to live. You know how it works: First you are presented with a list of important lifestyle parameters—the cost of living, the crime rate, the school system, the air quality, the climate, and so on. From these you select the ones you feel are the most important, the most valued. Plugging all of this data into a formula, you calculate your "best" option. Then, I guess, you pack up the car and move. The whole process reminds you of how you replaced your defunct washer-dryer with the help of *Consumer Reports*.

People rarely live in our major cities because they have made reasoned, sensible choices, based on a rational weighing of multiple criteria. They live here because very specific forces and factors brought them here and keep them here. Here is what I found.

The Five Major Reasons Why People Live in a Big City

1 It's where they were born
2 It's where they went to school
3 It's where the jobs are
4 They're young and plan on leaving later
5 They're old and can't leave

There is, of course, that small but enthusiastic group of people who actually prefer living in the city. But in most cases, it appears that the city chooses you rather than the other way around.

Confirming this impression was a survey I recently discovered conducted by *Country House* magazine. The editors queried their readers about their lifestyle preferences, asking, "If money were no object, where would you prefer to life?" The choices were:

(a) a mansion in Beverly Hills
(b) a four-bedroom Tudor in the suburbs
(c) a townhouse in Manhattan
(d) a farmhouse in the country, a few acres, and a pond

Everyone loved the farmhouse idea (not surprising, given the name of the magazine) and retreated from the cities (maybe it was the choices). Unconvinced by the results of this single survey, I sought a second opinion. I found a Gallup poll that canvassed a broader audience, asking them again: Where would they prefer to live? Money still not a factor, the preferred choice was living in a small town (34 percent), followed by the suburbs (24 percent), then the country (22 percent). Trailing the pack (19 percent)—you guessed it—was living in a major city.

It seems that big-city life is not everyone's cup of latte. For many, big-city living is an acquired taste. Visiting is one thing, but that's about it. You do not have to look far for the reasons why.

City Stress

People who don't live in big cities think of them as nerve-racking, chaotic, and demanding. Those of us who do live in big cities know the truth: They are right. When it comes to gripes and grievances, the city is a virtual gold mine. Yet when you ask people, "What are the stresses and strains you experience living in the city?" most come up with the same items. So here they are, the top ten most-often cited sources of stress in the city. Be warned, it's not pretty.

The Top Ten Stresses of the City

1 Crime	**6** Crowds
2 Unfriendliness	**7** Noise
3 Children's safety	**8** Poverty
4 Expense	**9** Filth
5 Traffic	**10** Pollution

If you look deeper, however, you can find more subtle sources of city stress.

- **The Uncertainty.** Once upon a time, most people lived in the country or in small towns. Life there had, and still has, a rhythm that is usually dependable and often predictable. Most days have a routine with a familiarity and sameness that can be either comforting or maddening. What you see is pretty much what you get. Life in a big city, however, is far less predictable. There is always something about to happen that we haven't planned for.

Living in a large city means always waiting for the other shoe to drop. Something unexpected is bound to happen, it's just a matter of time. It could be the dangers of the city, the demands of others, or merely the flaws of a system stretched to the limit. It can be as simple as waiting in a long line, being awakened at three in the morning by the wailing of a car alarm, or getting stuck in traffic and missing an important appointment. We never know completely what is going to happen next. We have little control. And having less control means feeling more stressed.

- **The Emotional Isolation.** One of the things I value about life in the city is the possibility of anonymity. There can be stretches of time when you do not bump into anyone you know or who knows you. It can be delicious if you desire it, or when it comes in measured doses. The downside is, you may not want it and cannot escape it.

Cities, by definition, are full of strangers. It's very likely that you will not know many of the people who live down the block or even in your building. These feelings of unconnectedness can foster a sense of isolation, especially in contrast to the hubbub of social activity taking place outside. The sad irony is that we often feel most alone when there are a lot of people around.

• **The Hassle.** When we think of stress, we usually think of the major stresses in our lives: becoming seriously ill, being mugged, or totaling the car. But there are, of course, those less dramatic stresses: catching a cold, losing your wallet, or merely denting the car. And if we look further, there are even smaller stresses: the mini-stresses and the micro-stresses. Much, if not most, of the stress we feel living in the city comes from these small but stressful situations and experiences. These constitute what we call "hassles." Here is but a taste of what the city has to offer.

- piles of take-out menus under your door
- pushing and shoving
- dog poop on the sidewalks
- elevators that never come
- potholes
- perfume pollution
- gridlock
- salesclerks with attitude
- overcrowded restaurants with less than an inch between tables
- clueless taxi drivers
- people bombarding you with handbills
- deliverymen who come "sometime between nine and five"
- sitting in traffic listening to the sound of a thousand horns
- beepers sounding in theaters, movies
- cell phones in restaurants

- cars that splash you
- smokers
- nonsmokers
- no taxis when you're late or it's raining
- broken parking meters
- noisy neighbors, thin walls
- squeegee guys at stoplights
- three buses in a row, then none just as you make it to the corner
- public telephones that eat quarters
- long lines and slow service
- no public washrooms
- filthy streets and people who litter
- car alarms misfiring
- reckless bicyclists
- hot, overcrowded subways and buses
- exact-change buses
- noisy garbage trucks early in the morning
- double-parkers
- panhandlers at ATMs
- looking for a parking place
- still looking for a parking place

When you take a closer look at city hassles you become aware of two things: First, there are *lots* of them; and second, they happen *over* and *over* again. Urban stress is largely the product of a succession of hassles. You can handle one, maybe even two, and possibly three or four. But when the number of hassles creeps higher, you can quickly become overwhelmed and feel defeated. Your plate fills, and with each additional hassle your overall distress level rises. The pent-up anger or upset that has slowly been building now erupts, and you overreact to a relatively unimportant problem or situation. That, of course, results in even more stress.

The funny part is, we usually deal fairly well with the bigger problems. Life's major stresses—the deaths, illnesses, divorces, or financial setbacks—somehow trigger hidden resources within us. We rise to each demand, summoning up some unknown inner strength, and we somehow manage to cope. What gets to us are the little things. It's the small stuff—the petty annoyances, small frustrations, and minor irritations—that ultimately produce a chronic sense of stress. It is the hassle of the city that becomes the real enemy. And too often, we pay the price.

The Effects of Urban Stress

The effects of stress can range from the subtle to the dramatic; from the benign to the downright scary. Here is a short list of possibilities:

THE BLUES	THE ACHES
Down	Backaches
Dejected	Headaches
Unhappy	Stomachaches

THE BLAHS	THE OVERS
Apathetic	Overeating
Listless	Overspending
Burnt out	Overeverything

It appears that in the city, as in life, there is no free brunch.

Some stress signs and symptoms affect us in less obvious ways. Here are some of the important indicators to watch out for:

• **The Hidden Stress.** The stress of life in a big city is much like an incessant background noise. You get used to it. There are periods of time when you do not even notice it, until it stops. We feel this absence of stress when we are not exposed to the city for a while. Something is different; you feel emotionally lighter. I become aware of this whenever I return to the city after a vacation. The reentry can be unsettling. Adjusting takes a bit of time.

The feeling is akin to wearing shoes that are a bit too tight. You get through the day pretty well, but when you take them off at night, you sure feel the difference. It's that sigh of relief that tells you something wasn't right. This hidden distress unconsciously telegraphs a sense of continuing apprehension or uneasiness, mild at times, overwhelming at others. These feelings hover over us like a cloud, never totally dissipating.

• **Dragging Your Tush.** The most common symptom of urban stress is fatigue. You feel tired. For some people this feeling seems constant, and this weariness robs you of much of the satisfaction and any joy your day might offer. As one of my patients put it, "My tush starts to drag around one o'clock and by six all I want to do is go home and veg in front of the TV."

You are tired for two main reasons. First, you probably do not get enough sleep. And even if you were to get enough, the quality of your sleep may be less than optimal. Secondly, the strains of the day can drain you physically, tightening your muscles and fatiguing your body. So even if you were well rested when you left the house, by the end of the day you are exhausted. The chances of your getting out and going dancing are pretty slim.

- **Shorter Fuses.** Irritability is the second most common symptom of urban stress. This may partially account for the widely accepted image of the city dweller as hostile, rude, and nasty. Let's face it, when you are tired and irritable you're not going to be a barrel of laughs.

Urban irritability goes beyond sleep deprivation. Living in the city lowers your ability to tolerate frustration and discomfort. Your fuse gets shorter. Small frustrations and annoyances, which at other times and in other places would not upset you, now get to you.

- **"We Don't Give a Damn."** Big cities have a reputation for fostering apathy and insensitivity. In general, this reputation is well earned. Some urbanites have elevated this "practiced indifference" to an art form. The exact origin of this behavior is unclear but I suspect it started in crowded elevators or on overcrowded buses where, when pressed next to each other, we were forced to pretend that we didn't notice the person at our elbow or on our foot. It is a defense that shields us from the imposed togetherness of the city and provides us with a modicum of privacy and separation. However, this defensive tactic can become internalized, and remain as a permanent pattern of behavior. Over time we become harder, tougher, and a lot less friendly.

Keep the City, Lose the Stress

As we can see, even at its gentlest, at its most benign, the city demands a lot from us. For some, leaving the city has been the answer.

These days it seems as if "the road less traveled" is clogged with fleeing urbanites. For others, the answer has been to stay but to minimize their interaction with the city as much as possible, insulating themselves from any potentially stressful encounter. They stay at home, retreat to their car, shun people, never go downtown, and certainly get out of town every weekend and every summer. These are genuine solutions; they will reduce your urban stress.

However, in their desire to de-stress their lives, these folks may be missing out on something. Our big cities can be wonderful places to live. Where else will you find the vitality, the energy, the cultural opportunities, the intellectual stimulation, and the diversity of people? Where else but in a big city can you have Lithuanian or Southern Latvian food delivered to your door? Where else can you hear five different languages spoken in the same coffee shop? And where else can you find a Cary Grant and a Hugh Grant movie playing on the same block?

In the pages that follow you will learn how to eliminate, or at least minimize, the *distressing* parts of city life while enjoying all the vibrancy, excitement, and joy that a big city has to offer. De-stressing your life need not mean throwing out the baby, too—even if the baby in question *is* particularly difficult.

2

Measuring Your Urban Stress

You are no bigger than the things that annoy you.

—JERRY BUNDSEN

The first steps in de-stressing your life in the city involve identifying what your stress looks like, where it comes from, and how it affects you. This chapter provides you with two stress indicators. Both measure your urban stress levels and your ability to cope with that stress. By completing each of the two brief scales below, you will have a clearer picture of the sources of your stress and of how much of that stress is self-induced.

Take a few minutes now to determine your scores. If you are not in a questionnaire mood, come back to this section later. But don't skip it entirely. Your scores are useful tools in helping you better understand and manage your urban stress. You can also retake these measures at a later time and see how your stress levels have changed as your ability to cope with the city improves.

YOUR URBAN STRESS LEVEL

This is a measure of the extent to which you perceive and experience the city as stressful. It indicates your Urban Triggers and assesses the impact these triggers have on you. It also provides you with a gauge of the broader impact of a variety of urban stresses and hassles.

For each of the potential stresses and hassles below, indicate the extent to which you feel they are stressful for you. Use this simple rating scale:

0 = Not a stress
1 = A minor stress
2 = A moderate stress
3 = A major stress

crime	____	congested traffic	____
dirty streets	____	inadequate parking spaces	____
overcrowding	____	inconsiderate drivers	____
the unfriendliness	____	smells	____
the homeless	____	rude people	____
the hurried pace	____	the high cost of living	____
graffiti	____	incompetent drivers	____
waiting in lines	____	frustrating public transit	____
not enough trees or grass	____	the quality of city's public schools	____
worry over children's safety	____	car break-ins	____
garbage on sidewalks	____	expensive parking	____
noise	____	expensive housing	____
polluted air	____	street hookers and druggies	____

mice, rats, or roaches	____	panhandlers	____
inconsiderate neighbors	____	car, truck, or bus fumes	____
foul street language	____	waiters and clerks with attitude	____
cramped living space	____	the pushing and shoving	____
lack of privacy	____	limited places for kids to play	____
		Your Urban Stress score	____

Rating Your Urban Stress Score

Your score is a measure of the extent to which you perceive the city to be stressful. Your rating indicates how your score compared with those of many other big-city dwellers. An Average rating, for example, means that your score fell within the same range as most other people. Above or Below Average means that you scored respectively higher or lower than most other people.

YOUR SCORE	YOUR URBAN STRESS LEVEL
90 and above	Much Above Average
60 to 89	Above Average
40 to 59	Average
10 to 39	Below Average
0 to 9	"Liar, liar, pants on fire."

You now have some idea of your overall stress level, at least that part of your stress that you attribute to the city. The question remains, however, of just how much of your stress is self-induced or at least exacerbated by your personality traits, lifestyle, and workstyle.

The questionnaire that follows determines your Hassle Quotient, or HQ. It is an index of your urban resilience, a measure of those personality traits and lifestyle habits that protect you from the stresses and strains of the big city.

First a word about questionnaires. I recognize that questionnaires and rating scales can be annoying and frustrating by their lack of specificity. Our emotional reactions rarely fall into simple, discrete "yes-no" categories, so there is rarely a simple, unqualified answer to most of the questions asked below. Try to answer each as best you can. Do not overanalyze. Do not overagonize.

YOUR HASSLE QUOTIENT (HQ)

For each item below, circle the response that best describes you. Don't worry about the numbers, simply remember that left to right means "more like me."

more like me→

	NOT AT ALL LIKE ME	ONLY A LITTLE LIKE ME	MODERATELY LIKE ME	VERY MUCH LIKE ME
1) I become impatient waiting in lines.	0	1	2	3
2) I worry too much about small stuff.	0	1	3	5
3) I generally feel well rested.	5	3	1	0
4) There are people I can confide in when I have a problem.	3	2	1	0
5) I handle rejection pretty well.	3	2	1	0
6) I get angry too easily.	0	1	2	3
7) I feel that I am not assertive enough.	0	1	2	3

8) Small inconveniences upset me more than they should.	0	1	3	5
9) Other people think I have a short fuse.	0	1	3	5
10) I get bored very easily.	0	1	2	3
11) I believe that in life, nice guys finish last.	0	1	3	5
12) I hold on to grudges far too long.	0	1	2	3
13) My social life is satisfying.	3	2	1	0
14) I get easily irritated by the stupidity of others.	0	1	3	5
15) I do some form of physical activity fairly regularly.	3	2	1	0
16) I often spend time with close friends.	3	2	1	0
17) I get upset when things go too slowly.	0	1	2	3
18) I'm pretty okay not knowing what's going to happen next.	3	2	1	0
19) I can easily laugh at myself.	5	3	1	0
20) I feel accepted and loved by family and friends.	3	2	1	0
21) I often see minor hassles as major problems.	0	2	3	5
22) I do not have much willpower.	0	1	2	3
23) I get into more than my share of arguments with people.	0	1	3	5
24) Most of the time I feel pretty good about myself.	3	2	1	0
25) I have a low tolerance for noise and commotion.	0	1	3	5

26) I get easily annoyed when I am stuck in traffic.	0	1	2	3
27) I worry a lot about being in an accident or getting sick.	0	1	2	3
28) I have hobbies and/or activities I enjoy.	3	2	1	0
29) I have good organizational skills.	5	3	1	0
30) I become stressed when I cannot control situations.	0	1	3	5
31) I hate it when someone gets the better of me.	0	1	2	3
32) I have good time-management skills.	5	3	2	0
33) Most of the time I am in a good mood.	3	2	1	0
34) I can see the funny side of situations.	5	3	1	0
35) I am a highly competitive person.	0	1	2	3
36) I handle uncertainty and change pretty well.	3	2	1	0
37) Other people's rudeness makes me very angry.	0	1	3	5
38) People who know me would say I am easygoing.	5	3	1	0
39) I generally stay pretty cool when things get crazy.	3	2	1	0
40) I hate confrontations with others.	0	1	2	3
41) My feelings are easily hurt.	0	1	3	5

Column totals: _____ _____ _____ _____

Your total score: _____

Rating Your HQ

YOUR HQ	YOUR RATING
100+	Very Stress Producing
75 to 100	Stress Producing
65 to 74	Borderline
35 to 64	Stress Effective
0 to 34	Very Stress Effective

Understanding Your Scores

These scores tell you something about the way you experience the stress of life in a big city. Your Urban Stress level is a measure of which city stresses get to you and how much stress they produce. It measures your stress triggers. The higher your score, the more stress you are reporting. An elevated score may come from having many small stresses, several major stresses, or both.

Your HQ is a measure of your personal vulnerability, the extent to which you create even more stress than is appropriate. It assesses your level of frustration tolerance, aspects of your self-esteem, how demanding you are, your expectations, your psychological coping skills, and your lifestyle management skills. A high HQ suggests that life in the city for you will be more of an uphill battle than it should be. The lower your HQ, the better you are able to cope with urban pressures and urban demands. Lowering your HQ is one of the more important ways of reducing your level of Urban Stress.

While each score is of interest in itself, it is the combination of the two scores that best characterizes the ways you manage or fail to manage the demands and frustrations of city life. Chances are, your scoring pattern will resemble one of three "Urban Stress Styles." Try to determine which stress style below best describes you.

Urban Stress Style #1

The Urbanite

SCORE PROFILE

- Average or Below Average Urban Stress Level
- Low Hassle Quotient

This is the profile you should be aiming for.

This urban profile describes someone who is not overly stressed by his or her life in a big city. Sure there are some aspects and features of city life that are stressful, but they aren't excessive in number and the amount of stress that they trigger is limited. Here we see a relatively good "urban fit," a positive match between the demands of the urban environment, the needs, styles, and preferences of the individual, and his or her psychological coping skills.

The Urbanite is not delighted with all the hassle and stress that come with life in the city, is not a Pollyanna, nor is he or she naive. The Urbanite is able to cope with most of the pressures, demands, and frustrations of city life in an adaptive manner.

Urban Stress Style #2

The Urban Mismatch

SCORE PROFILE

- Above Average Urban Stress Level
- Low Hassle Quotient

Linda, a former patient of mine, was an Urban Mismatch. Her Urban Stress Level was fairly high, while her Hassle Quotient was relatively low. She perceived the city as stressful, and she was feeling that stress. Yet her psychological resilience was fairly high. She had excellent coping skills.

Linda disliked the big city. And not without reason. Her downtown apartment was small and dreary, her neighborhood was dirty and not terribly safe, and her job was predictable and boring. She seemed to spend most of her workdays in elevators and subway trains. In her windowless office it often felt like days would go by without her seeing the sun. It was clearly not where she wanted to be. Linda remained in the city only for her job. In two years she would be able to move to a part of the country where she would be happier, a place with lots of empty space, open sky, and fresh air. At heart, she was a country mouse.

As a classic Urban Mismatch, Linda found herself in a dislikable situation under disagreeable conditions. For her it was simply a case of "When wrong places happen to good people."

Underlying the stress of any Urban Mismatch is a poor fit between the individual and the setting. Whenever a person and his or her environment don't click, a certain amount of stress is inevitable. Linda's low HQ indicated that her psychological and practical coping skills were fairly good. She was unhappy about living in a big city. Not everyone likes big-city life, and this is fine. Being unhappy with life in the big city need not be viewed as a character flaw or lack of flexibility on anyone's part. One can legitimately prefer not to be exposed to congestion, pollution, noise, and crowds.

However, if you find yourself chronically stressed about life in the city, and if you find that even on those days when the city is on its best behavior you are still unhappy, upset, angry, tense, nervous, sleepless, or feel any of the other common stress signs and symptoms, there may be something else going on. You may be a UC.

Urban Stress Style #3

The Unhappy Camper

SCORE PROFILE

- Elevated Urban Stress Level
- High Hassle Quotient

The Unhappy Camper has a hard time with life in the city. But unlike the Urban Mismatch, the reasons are more complicated than merely a poor fit. The Unhappy Camper is unhappy about too many things too much of the time.

Judith was an Unhappy Camper. She felt besieged, and most days she went to war. There was the battle of the bus, the battle of the crowds, the battle of the noise, and of course that neverending battle, the battle with "other people." Clashes and skirmishes abounded. Unfortunately, she was losing most of the battles.

Classic UCs have too many buttons. They allow themselves to be stressed by circumstances and events that should be viewed as minor or insignificant. The Unhappy Camper fights too hard too often. They feel drained, emotionally and physically.

But it is not just the city that triggers this stress. Classic UCs—and you may be one of them—get irritated, upset, and frustrated too easily by many other aspects of their lives that have nothing to do with living in a big city. For them, living in another environment wouldn't relieve the frustration. Similar levels of stress would remain. For UCs, reducing stress means self-change rather than changing what's "out there." It means changing the ways in which they react to frustration, disapproval, rejection, and disappointment.

Changing Your Stress Style

The good news is that you can change the way you think and feel, and you can certainly change the ways in which you live your life in the city. If you are a Mismatch or a UC or a combination, the real question you want answered is "How do I make my life in the city more satisfying?" The answer lies in learning how to reduce the number of Urban Triggers in your life and/or how to become more emotionally resilient and able to cope more effectively with the stresses. The remaining chapters will show you how to do both. After you have applied some of the ideas and suggestions, come back and retake these measures and see how your Urban Stress Style has changed.

3

Developing Urban Attitude

He who laughs, lasts.

—MARY PETTIBONE POOLE

*O*ne morning, out of the blue, I got a call from my sister in Canada who had some wonderful news. Michael, our nephew, had been accepted to a graduate school in New York. Could we put him up for a while until he found a place of his own? Absolutely, I said. We'd be delighted.

About a week later there was a second call, this time from friends upstate whose daughter Karen had just been offered a job in the city. She needed someplace to stay while she looked for a place to live. Could we? Of course. We were doubly delighted.

Watching them adjust and react to the city proved interesting and illuminating. As it turned out, Michael loved the city, and Karen, well, though she didn't hate it, certainly wasn't having much fun. She was constantly struggling, fighting the city every step of the way. Regularly Karen would report back to us detailing fresh irritations, upsets, and aggravations. For her, the city was a stressful battleground in a war she was clearly losing. Michael, on the other hand, found adapting to city life relatively easy. He was able to roll with the punches, taking the frustrations and annoyances of the city in stride.

Two people, same city, similar stresses, yet very different reactions. How come?

Triggers and Buttons

Feeling stressed is, and always has been, a two-part process: You need a trigger and a button. You need something external to trigger a stress reaction, and something within you that determines just how strong your reaction will be.

Urban Triggers are all the potential stresses and hassles of city life. They can be events, situations, circumstances, other people—just about anything. They range from the minor, such as a rude salesclerk or not finding a place to park—to the serious—being mugged or assaulted, for example. The city has an inexhaustible supply of triggers. Even on a slow day the city can produce enough triggers to fill the biggest plate.

Your stress buttons are a measure of your vulnerability to a stress trigger. You know you have a stress button if a particular stress "gets to you." What characterizes stress buttons are their size and their number. If you are feeling only a little stress, your button is small. If you are in great emotional pain or are sporting a headache the size of New Jersey, your button is a big one. The bigger the button, the more quickly you will react to the associated stress trigger and the greater the impact will be. Having lots of buttons means you are susceptible to a large number of Urban Stresses. You are an easy target. The city will find you and get you.

Urban Teflon

The key to becoming stress resilient is developing something I call "urban attitude." No, urban attitude is *not* that haughty look your prima donna of a waiter gave you when you asked him politely to repeat the dinner specials. Nor is it that snotty smirk from that cad who stole your taxi. No, that's simply behaving like a jerk. Urban attitude is something *good,* something you want to have.

Urban attitude consists of a number of specific attitudes and psychological skills that foster a high degree of stress resilience. It changes the way you perceive the city and the ways in which you react to the stresses of the city. It is your Teflon coating. Michael has it, and hopefully Karen will get it. This chapter will show you how you can develop urban attitude.

THE SIMPLE LITTLE SYSTEM

Much of our Urban Stress involves some form of overreaction. The importance of any stressful incident or situation can be dwarfed by the magnitude of our emotional response. Take last Friday for example, my *bad hair* day.

After frantically rushing to pick up our daughter from school and dropping her off at home, I raced to my hair salon for my three-thirty appointment. Arriving in the nick of time, I discovered that the client before me was not yet finished. I nicely asked Angela, my stylist, if I should come back a little later. "No," she said, "stick around. It'll be just a few more minutes." It wasn't. I waited. And then I waited some more. I was becoming annoyed. I was not happy.

I was overreacting. There were no pressing plans or appointments that I would miss. The time I had to wait was not outrageous, there were things to read, and Angela is a real sweetie. Yet my stress level was out of whack. I was off balance.

One of the secrets of stress control is achieving and maintaining stress balance. This simple little system can quickly help you assess whether you are overreacting to stressful situations.

Step One: Rate Your Stress Level

First, rate the *amount of stress* you are feeling about a particular stressful episode using this ten-point scale.

10
9 I was extremely distressed
8
7
6 I was moderately distressed
5
4
3 I was only a little distressed
2
1
0 Not distressed at all

"Distress" here can mean any one of many stress emotions—anger, upset, annoyance, sadness, disappointment, frustration, worry, aggravation, and the like. My stress level, in this case my annoyance at having to wait, was probably a four.

Step Two: Rate the Relative Importance of the Stress

Whenever you experience some stress, attempt to identify the source of your stress and rate its relative importance on a similar ten-point scale. Use this Stress-Importance Scale.

10
9 Major importance
8
7
6 Moderate importance
5
4
3 Minor importance
2
1
0 Not important at all

To help you get the feel of the scale, think of three *major* stresses that could happen or have happened to you. These are your nines and tens, the serious life-altering events that we dread and hope will never happen.

1. _____ 2. _____ 3. _____

If you are having trouble coming up with anything, you might consider these unfortunate possibilities: death of a loved one, major financial loss, life-threatening illness, loss of your job, chronic pain. Not a pleasant list! Compared to these, my having to wait for a haircut would probably rate a one.

Step Three: Evaluate Your Stress Balance

Now simply ask yourself: **"Does the stress I am feeling match the importance of the situation?"**

If it does not, you are off balance. Your stress level is out of line. I was off balance when I had a four reaction to a one situation. So was my neighbor when he became overly angry about his newspaper arriving in less than mint condition. Similarly, my daughter's hysteria when she learned that her favorite shirt was in the laundry, and my son's great upset when he was told that he had to clean his room this month, were all off balance. In each case there was too much stress. These problems, situations, and circumstances do not deserve this kind of emotional investment. Knowing you are off balance tells you that you are overreacting to a situation. Your button is bigger than it has to be, and you are causing yourself more stress than is necessary.

To help you master this process, complete this exercise. How would you rate your potential *stress level* and the *importance level* if confronted with the following urban situations?

	YOUR STRESS LEVEL	THE IMPORTANCE LEVEL
• Caught in traffic (no major appointments).	_____	_____
• Salesclerk serves someone before you, even though you were there first.	_____	_____

- Someone cuts you off on the road.   _____ _____

- Your waiter is taking forever to get to your   _____ _____
  table.

- You just miss your bus home. (Another will be   _____ _____
  along in five minutes.)

- You leave your wallet in a taxi.   _____ _____

You get the idea. If you are off balance, you are probably causing yourself more stress than is necessary. Whenever you feel stressed there is a very good chance that you are distorting or misrepresenting the event or situation that is triggering your stress. Here's what you have to do to regain your stress balance.

CHANGING YOUR PERCEPTIONS

In many ways the stress of the city is like a Rorschach, or inkblot test. What you see and how you experience the city reflects who you are and how you look at the city. Whenever you take any group of people and expose them to the same stress or hassle, chances are you will get a range of reactions. What is mildly annoying to one person may mean nothing to a second, and possibly incite a third to violence.

I have always felt that much, if not most, of our stress is self-created. Learning how to perceive the city and its demands differently is the key to a stress-effective urban lifestyle. Your attitudes and beliefs about any potentially stressful situation or event determine how much stress you will experience. Look at something one way and you feel major stress; look at it another way and you feel less or maybe even no stress. In short: same city, different take.

Most urban hassles, be they traffic jams, deranged panhandlers, nasty clerks, miserable landlords, dirty streets, or bad service in overcrowded restaurants, do not in themselves have the power to create stress. We empower these situations with the ways in which we view them. If you change that perception, you can eliminate, or certainly diminish, the amount of stress you feel. And you *can* change the way you look at things.

Stop "Catastrophizing" and "Awfulizing"

We have a very strong tendency to exaggerate, perceiving common hassles as catastrophes. On any day, in fact on most days, we easily make a molehill into something much larger. "Catastrophizing" and "awfulizing" are certainly the most common forms of such emotional exaggeration. Let me show you how they work.

1. Pick a hassle, any hassle. This can be any common city annoyance from our hassle list, such as being stuck in downtown traffic.
2. Now for the fun part. Say to yourself: "Oh my God, this is the worst thing that could happen! It's just awful! It's terrible!" It adds to the effect if you can manage to summon up a pained look while you are saying this. Frequent sighing is good, too.

By elevating a hassle to a tragedy or a catastrophe, we also elevate our emotional levels. We can quickly move from mere annoyance to homicidal intent. The reality is, unless you are late for your

Nobel Prize award ceremony or a real emergency is at hand, being stuck in traffic—and most of the other items on our hassle list—are *only* hassles, minor annoyances, disappointments, and frustrations, and should be perceived as such.

Even the more serious stresses can easily be magnified, becoming much more stressful than they have to be. Leaving your wallet in the cab, losing your keys, having your neighbor keep you up half the night, are *still* not major life crises, although at that moment you may think they are.

Here are two helpful questions you can ask yourself if you are unsure as to whether you are catastrophizing or awfulizing:

1. How important is this *really*? (Remember your nines and tens.)
2. Will I remember this in three years, three months, in three weeks, or in three days (or even in three hours!)?

Minimize Your "Can't-stand-it-itis"

"Can't-stand-it-itis," which may sound like a rare transmittable disease, is simply another form of emotional exaggeration. We cause this distortion whenever we start with an "I don't like it" and turn it into an "I can't stand it!"

Even though you may not *like* the hassles and frustrations of the city, you do not have to go ballistic and explode with inflated rage. "I just *hate* it when I am in traffic!!! (or crowds, lines, rude people, etc. . . .)" The difference is more than semantic. When you really believe you *can't stand* something, you produce a great deal of internal stress, far more than is warranted by the situation or circumstance. You make yourself very upset, angry, and distraught. You can quickly turn a one- or two-level trigger into a seven or eight stress response.

At the heart of this form of exaggeration is something called "Low Frustration Tolerance," or LFT for short. We see LFT in the two-year-old who, when denied more cookies, has a tantrum. Much of the type of LFT displayed by the two-year-old is still with us.

Unfortunately, living in a big city means living with a great deal of frustration. So you have a choice: You can fume and get yourself into an emotional stew, with "I can't stand this" and "I can't stand that," or you can try another route. When you recognize that can't-stand-it-itis is contributing to your emotional overreaction, step back and ask yourself:

- Can I really not stand it, or do I really mean I don't like it?
- Couldn't I really stand it for quite a bit longer? And if some guy was willing to fork over really big bucks, couldn't I stand this for maybe even longer?
- Is my overreacting here helping me in any way? Or is it really making things worse?

Stop "Overgeneralizing"

Following are some examples of "overgeneralizing" heard in the city.

- "Nobody in this city gives a damn about anybody else!" (You find that someone has swiped your morning newspaper.)
- "The people in this city simply do not know how to drive!" (Someone has cut you off in traffic.)
- "The city is run by morons!" (After having been put on hold

with the Department of Motor Vehicles for ten minutes, the line goes dead.)

Now I am not suggesting that there is *no* truth to these assertions. While there is no doubt that *some* people fit into these categories, many more do not. By overgeneralizing we create a distorted picture of the city and its inhabitants and in the process add more stress to our lives. Whenever we think in terms of all or nothing, black or white, good or bad, right or wrong, we wind up a little less happy in the city and in life.

To help you curb any tendency to overgeneralize, here are some useful ideas:

- Ask yourself if you are focusing on only one small part of a person's overall behavior, and too quickly assuming that this sample truly characterizes that person as a whole.
- Try to think of individuals or situations that do *not* fit into your overgeneralization.
- Look out for language that reflects this all-or-nothing thinking. Watch for words like "always" and "never," as in "People in the city are *never* friendly" or "People *always* take advantage of you when they have the chance."

The reality is, cities and the people who live in them exist on a continuum. Find the gray areas.

Check for "What-ifing"

If you are having a slow day in a big city, here are some of the things you can worry about.

- What if I'm walking down the street and a piece of a building falls on me!
- What if the subway breaks down!
- What if I fall down a manhole!
- What if the transit strike lasts for a whole year!
- What if my car breaks down in the middle of downtown at rush hour!
- What if my waiter has some kind of disease!
- What if I get hit by a car!
- What if I get rock musicians as new neighbors!
- What if my taxi driver is a serial killer!
- What if a plane falls on my house!
- What if I inhale polluted air!
- What if I get food poisoning!
- What if the guy behind me at the ATM is a mugger!
- What if the bus driver is on drugs!
- What if I'm kidnapped!
- What if I'm murdered!
- What if the world ends!

If you live in a big city, a lot can happen that you do not want to happen. Things get fouled up easily and the results can prove upsetting and frustrating. The city gives you a lot to worry about. Can these things happen? You bet. Will they? Probably not. The truth is, most of the things we worry about happening, never happen. And even if they do, they probably won't be the tragedies we predict.

Many of us are "What-ifers." Whenever we what-if, we take a situation or event that *could* happen and make it into something that probably *will* happen. This way of looking at the world can and will cause you much unnecessary stress.

I remember the worries voiced by one particular participant in one of my Stress in the City workshops. She was clearly a major-league what-ifer. She worried: "What if it gets really hot this summer?" Following up on this thought, she reasoned, "When it gets hot, I will be forced to turn on the air-conditioning." Then she worried: "What if the a/c leaks as it has in the past and the floor underneath buckles?" Should it buckle, she would be forced to contact the super, whom she thinks hates her guts. "What if he sees the damage?" This will give him the ammunition to get her. "What if I get evicted? Where will I go?"

What if, what if, what if . . .

Assess Your Control

A sense of not having control can easily trigger stress, because we tend to feel uncertain. In turn, feeling uncertain can create feelings of anxiety and upset. Becoming more comfortable with uncertainty and a lack of control is an essential ingredient of urban attitude.

The first step in becoming more comfortable with not having control is recognizing the *extent* of your control. This short exercise will help you assess your control capabilities.

To what extent can you control these events or circumstances? Put an X at that point on the line that best describes the amount of control you feel you have about each of the following items.

	NO CONTROL	→ →	TOTAL CONTROL
1. The weather in the city	__ __ __ __	__ __	__ __ __ __
2. Selecting the personnel working in shops and stores	__ __ __ __	__ __	__ __ __ __

3. The speed of elevators   — — — — — — — — —
4. City traffic   — — — — — — — — —
5. Other people's obnoxious   — — — — — — — — —
   personalities
6. The cleanliness of the city   — — — — — — — — —
7. Streamlining the city's   — — — — — — — — —
   bureaucracy
8. Preventing people from acting   — — — — — — — — —
   like morons
9. The crime rate   — — — — — — — — —
10. The amount of noise on city   — — — — — — — — —
    streets

The point of the exercise, of course, is to illustrate just how limited we can be when it comes to controlling our environment and those in it. Philosophic acceptance of our inability to control the many situations and behaviors that occur around us, especially if we live in the city, becomes an important skill to master.

The next time you find yourself in a potentially stressful situation ask yourself: "How much control do I really have in this situation?" If your answer is "Not much," ask yourself a second question: "Then why am I making myself so stressed?"

Expect the Expected

Our expectations play an important role in determining how we react to a stressful situation. If your expectations are unrealistic, there is a good chance you will overreact. Try this simple five-item test to see how realistic your expectations are about life in a big city.

The Urban Expectations Test

Simply circle the answer that best fits what you would expect to happen in the following situations.

1. You are waiting in the express checkout aisle of a supermarket and the person in front of you has fifteen items, clearly violating the ten-item limit. You ask him to use the more appropriate aisle. He replies:

(a) "You got a problem with this?"

(b) "My purchases fall within the same four food groups, therefore I actually have fewer than ten."

(c) "Oh my gosh, you're right! What could I have been thinking? I will immediately move to the correct line. Thank you for pointing this out to me."

2. Your rent has been raised by a ridiculous amount, so you tell the landlord that he is pond scum and that you are moving out. You begin looking for something else and

(a) find it is a tougher market than you imagined, but you do find something at twice the cost and half the size.

(b) after weeks of not seeing anything you would even remotely consider—and everything is at sickening prices—you crawl back to your old landlord and beg him to let you stay.

(c) you quickly find a place that is half the rent, much bigger, and has a terrace, a river view, a roof garden, and fundamentalist neighbors who have taken a vow of silence.

3. You are in a taxi and the driver is driving far too fast. You ask him to slow down. He says:

(a) Nothing. He does not understand the language.

(b) "Relax! I am a trained professional."

(c) "Golly, I must not have been paying attention. I will slow down immediately. I appreciate your concern, and I am so sorry! You can be darn sure this won't happen again."

4. You drop your family off in front of the restaurant and say you will join them in a moment or two after you find a parking spot. You wave good-bye and

(a) after searching for a spot for fifteen minutes you pull into a lot and pay the attendant $12.50.

(b) you drive around and around for forty-five minutes with no luck, not even a parking lot. You park in front of a hydrant and arrive back at the restaurant in time to see the others finishing dessert and coffee.

(c) you proceed, driving but a half block away and notice three vacant spots. One of them has enough money in the meter to keep it ticking well into next year. You park, turn off the engine, and beat your family to the table.

5. You are getting on a crowded bus when the person behind starts pushing you in a frantic attempt to get on. You complain, "You are crushing my arm! There's no more room!" The other person responds:

(a) "If you'd lose a few pounds, chubby, we'd all get on!"

(b) "Keep your lips closed, doodle-brain!"

(c) "Indeed I am, and for that I am truly sorry! You are right; this bus is more than full and the best thing I could do would be to step off and catch the next one. I would like to apologize for my rudeness to you and to all others on this bus for my totally unacceptable behavior. Have a good day."

You picked c's? Fuhgeddaboutit!

Other bits of dialogue you should never expect to hear while living in a big city:

- "Thank God I finally caught up to you! By any chance did this twenty-dollar bill fall out of your pocket about three blocks ago?"
- "That disheveled and disgusting man lying in the street may not be a drunk. I'll see if I can help him. Could you help me by calling for some police assistance?"
- "I couldn't possibly accept that ten dollars for helping you open that window. After all, as your super, that's my job."
- "I'd like to apologize for my dog's barking this morning. I now realize I may have to give him up and get a cat."
- "I know we promised you delivery at nine. I am calling to say we are sorry but we won't be able to make it till about nine-thirty."
- "Yes we certainly can deliver your new bed. Six flights? No elevator? No problem. No, no extra charge."
- "Yes, of course your table is ready. Come right this way."
- "Why don't *you* take this parking spot? I happen to have some extra time today."
- "Sir, do you know where there is a trash receptacle? I have been carrying this gum wrapper for the last eight blocks."
- "Thank you."
- "You're welcome."

Curb Your Shoulds

Living in a big city, "unrealistic shoulds and shouldn'ts" can add appreciably to your stress level. Some examples:

- People *should* be more considerate of the needs of others!
- People *shouldn't* push and shove in crowds!
- He *shouldn't* have taken my parking spot!
- He *should* be more careful where he is walking!

But, you say, all this sounds pretty sensible. People *shouldn't* push, shove, butt in, and steal parking spots. People *should be* more careful and more considerate. That would be nice. But the reality is, they *do* act in these unmannerly and inconsiderate ways. There would be no problem here if we merely kept our shoulds and shouldn'ts as simple preferences. That is, "I would really *like* it if people were nicer." Or, "It certainly would be a better world if people were more considerate." However, we quickly convert a "should" to a "must" or a strict demand, and when others fail to heed that demand we condemn them as bad. We feel anger and resentment.

It is much like waking up one morning, discovering that it is raining, and complaining, "It *shouldn't* be raining!" The reality is, it *is* raining! Similarly, I can insist and demand that I be a few inches taller, or that I be unconscionably rich, or that my tennis game rival that of Andre Agassi. As angry or insistent as I get, it just isn't going to happen.

Usually we recognize the absurdity of these demands when it comes to noninterpersonal situations. However, when it comes to the actions of other people we fail to recognize that they continue to act in unappealing ways for a variety of reasons. It could be because they are a little bit neurotic, they are not terribly bright, or, more commonly, they have a different set of priorities than we do.

Whenever you find yourself using a should or shouldn't, ask yourself if you are being realistic. Is your "should" really a disguised "must" or a "have-to"? Then ask yourself, "Why *must* other people act the way I want them to?" And firmly tell yourself, "They don't, and often won't."

Play the Urban Cynic

Am I suggesting you become a tad cynical? Yes, to some extent. When you live in a big city there is a definite place for a healthy degree of cynicism. However, there is a big difference between a true cynic and an Urban Cynic. The true cynic believes the big city really is a place where aggravation and trouble are just around the next corner. The Urban Cynic, on the other hand, does not expect aggravation, trouble, and inconsideration, but is not surprised when it turns up. I prefer to think of it as a form of adaptive skepticism; a mind-set that knows that there are minefields out there but also knows that the chances of stepping on more than one or two in any week is remote. Beneath the skin of an Urban Cynic beats the heart of a streetwise optimist. The Urban Cynic has an eye open for the worst, but hopes to see the best.

Know What Matters Most

In the city, as in life, you quickly discover that a great deal of your stress comes from investing too much time and energy chasing after the wrong things. The goals and values we choose ultimately determine what upsets and worries us. Too often we do not choose wisely. If you live in a big city there is ample inducement and opportunity to take the kind of job and create the kind of life that are exhausting and unsatisfying. Meaningless work, killer hours, a toxic boss, neurotic clients, huge expenses, and too little time for friends and family—all can result in feelings of great stress. And too often it is the city that becomes the fall guy.

The real culprit may be your own sense of misplaced priorities. Daily I see people who yearn to escape the stresses of the city. Yet when I listen to them carefully, I realize that the city is not their problem. Many hate their jobs and resent the amount of time they have to spend at work. Many are dissatisfied with the way they live and what they have come to value. Many wrongfully conclude that the city is the enemy and decide to abandon it, when in reality the real stress is a workstyle and associated lifestyle they dislike or even detest.

We pay a high price when we buy into a lifestyle that fails to reflect what is important. While your job title and the size of your paycheck can be powerful incentives, it is important not to equate *what* you do and *how busy* you are with *who* you are. Failing to distinguish appropriately between *wanting* something and *needing* it, we quickly discover that we must work harder and longer to buy the things we *think* we really must have. In life there is very little we need beyond air, food, water, and shelter. And whatever else we might need probably does not include designer clothing, a house on the shore, putting our child into the city's best nursery school, or hobnobbing with the upper crust. We become the trapped prisoners of our own misguided values and high-maintenance lifestyle. The irony is, with all this work, effort, and sacrifice, many do not have the time or energy to enjoy the things their money buys them.

So before you call the movers, ask yourself this: How much of my stress would I take with me if I left the city? If your answer is "lots," you may want to start re-evaluating what is truly important and necessary for your life in the city to become more satisfying, more rewarding—and less stressful.

And Lighten Up

Here is a seven-item quiz that will help you assess the extent to which your style, pace, and personality fit the profile of a seasoned big-city dweller. Simply circle the letter that best describes your lifestyle preference:

1. My life would be much happier, if only
   (a) those I love were healthy and happy.
   (b) I had more money.
   (c) there was a Gap or Benetton in my neighborhood.

2. I believe this world would be a better place if only
   (a) people would be more considerate of others.
   (b) we could just learn how to better tolerate differences and diversity.
   (c) people would just mind their own damn business and leave-me-alone-thank-you!

2. I like my coffee
   (a) on the terrace, by a pool, served by a waiter in a little black jacket.

(b) in bed, with croissants, served by my loving family.

(c) in a paper cup, from a brown bag, purchased at a take-out deli.

4. I think that having a lot of stress and aggravation in your life
   (a) can rob you of much of life's joy.
   (b) can be harmful to your health.
   (c) is a great asset in helping you maintain your ideal weight.

5. The greatest invention of modern times is
   (a) the broad-spectrum antibiotic.
   (b) the personal computer.
   (c) the take-out menu.

6. If I had one wish, it would be
   (a) world peace.
   (b) an end to world hunger.
   (c) that my upstairs neighbor die a slow and painful death while his stupid stereo is on full blast.

7. What I really could use most in my life right now is
   (a) winning the lottery.
   (b) a long vacation, preferably in the south of France.
   (c) a third Starbucks opening up on my block.

Scoring

In each case, the correct answer is (c).

A total score of six or seven suggests that you are a metropolitan natural, a perfect urban fit. A score of three, four, or five suggests definite urban potential, but don't sell the farm just yet. Anything below a three . . . , well, let's say you may not be ready just yet to appreciate the delights of the urban experience.

If you take life in the big city too seriously, your goose is cooked. Over-seriousness can result in your giving too much power and importance to the idiosyncrasies, hassles, and all-too-frequent lunacy of urban life. Learn to laugh. Humor gives you the ability to defuse much of the potential stress and pressure all around you. If you can find a way of looking at a potentially stressful situation in ways that make you smile, you dilute the negative impact of that experience. A sharp sense of the absurd combined with a dash of whimsy can make your life in the city far more livable.

PART TWO

Stress Relief Strategies

4

Creating an Urban Oasis

As any modern city dweller knows, it's a million times simpler (if less virtuous) to live in a downtown metropolis than it is to eke out an existence in the bug-infested woods.

—MICHIKO KAKUTANI

*R*ecently I was skimming the Home section of my newspaper when I came across a photograph that made my jaw drop. The picture and the accompanying story illustrated perfectly, to the point of parody, the notion of creating a simpler, less stressful environment within a complex urban setting. Here, right in the middle of Manhattan, perched high atop a modern high-rise, was this woodsy-looking log cabin. This simple-looking structure, seemingly snatched from the back woods of Maine, was nestled amid the tallest buildings in the world. Reading further, I learned that this simple cabin was far from simple and wasn't snatched from anywhere. Painstakingly designed and tastefully decorated (Ralph Lauren, his Country collection), this rustic cabin cost somebody a bundle. It was someone's expensive fantasy brought to life. I must admit, as absurd and inappropriate as it looked, I loved this improbable urban oasis.

If you live in a big city, you need an oasis. The more stressful the city becomes, the more you need a refuge. The place where you live should be a retreat, sheltering you from the chaos and confusion surrounding it. Of course, it need not be as outlandish as this designer cabin or in a neighborhood as chic. But where you live should be an island of sanity and comfort, a place where you can unwind, regroup, and relax. Your neighborhood should impart a sense of safety, security, and community. When you open your front door, whether coming in or going out, you should feel serene, content, and at peace. This chapter shows you how you can create *your* oasis in the city.

FINDING YOUR CORNER

A neighborhood is where, when you go out of it, you get beat up.
—MURRAY KEMPTON (quoting a city office worker)

No one has ever mistaken our neighborhood for a Shaker village. This does not surprise us. Our neighborhood is always busy and never completely quiet. There is a constant whirl of activity and a perpetual background buzz. Yet our neighborhood is relatively peaceful compared to the other parts of the city. The pace of our neighborhood is slower, the crowds smaller, and the people seem friendlier. When we return home at the end of the day, we can feel the tension and stress beginning to ebb as our streets, shops, and homes come into view and the faces we see are ones we know.

Your neighborhood should be a place you feel good about. This means finding something more than a house or an apartment near a video store and a Chinese restaurant. You are looking for a neighborhood that offers a feeling of belonging, a sense of emotional security, *and* a video store and a Chinese restaurant. You want to live in a neighborhood that thrives.

The seemingly contradictory term "urban village" best captures what you are looking for. The "urban" part suggests complexity, intensity, options, and excitement—the best of what the city has to offer. Unfortunately it also connotes hostility, indifference, danger, and discomfort. That is why you need the "village" part. You also want simplicity, familiarity, and tranquillity. You want them all.

Urban villages that worked in the past were created by the immigrant families who settled in our bigger cities several generations ago. They brought with them a sense of village, and a sense of belonging to a neighborhood and a community that was intimate and supportive. We, too, should seek the same qualities in the modern city. We want all the positive things the city has to offer and the livability of a smaller town or village. The key to having them both lies in your choice of neighborhood.

Be Prepared to Shop Around

Location, location, location. That time-worn pearl of real estate financial wisdom may also be one of the secrets of stress-resilient living in the city. But to find that right corner you have to shop for your neighborhood. Too many people make the mistake of choosing their neighborhood without considering just how important it will be in determining their daily dose of stress.

My own wife was one of the people who made this mistake. When she came to New York from Chapel Hill, North Carolina, Beth was enticed by the smooth talk of an eager Realtor to rent a small apartment right in the busiest part of the city. The apartment was fine, but the neighborhood was chaotic. She said it felt as if she were living in Bloomingdale's (which was not far away). There was no feeling of community or a sense of belonging to a neighborhood. It was 100 percent urban, without the "village" part. Beth's mistake was that she didn't shop around.

To be a smart shopper you need to look at the city differently. Rather than seeing the city as one large chunk of realty, try to see it as a patchwork of neighborhoods and communities. Each neighborhood has its own personality, style, and level of appeal. Unlike the suburbs or even a small town, neighborhoods in a big city can vary dramatically. In many large cities, moving even a few blocks can put you in a very different environment and cause a dramatic change in the way you experience life in the city.

Ask some questions and do some legwork. Be bold. Be brazen. Ask people who know the city well what they think of the neighborhood you are considering. Ask friends and acquaintances if they know anyone who lives in that neighborhood. Ask for their phone numbers, and call them.

Most of all, spend time in the neighborhoods you are considering. Go there and talk to people who live there. If you are married, have children, are single, gay, vegetarian, a jogger, a dog owner, or you lean toward political fanaticism—whatever—see if there are a few like-minded individuals in the neighborhood.

Don't Make This Mistake

Many people, especially if they are new to the city, fall victim to the "Urban Fallacy." Simply stated, it holds:

It doesn't really matter that much *where* I live in the city, because I will make use of the entire city.

Wrong. It is easy to fall into this trap because we always start out with intentions more ambitious than are ever realized. Though we think, "The city will be my playground," and believe that we will spend much if not most of our time away from where we live—and we should—we do not. The reality is, after an initial honeymoon, other than going to work, most people find themselves becoming more reluctant to leave their own neighborhoods.

The general rule of thumb is: Think close. If a destination is not close to where you live, you are less likely to go there.

Look for Signs of Life

Street life is the pulse of a neighborhood. One index of the health and vitality of a neighborhood is the number of people you see on the street, especially on the weekends. Streets in the city that are *too* quiet may not be what you are looking for. You want to see your neighbors from time to time (some of them, anyway), even if you do not want them as best friends.

When Karen found a place of her own to live in the city she chose a neighborhood that really wasn't a neighborhood. The area was dominated by commercial office buildings whose inhabitants would disappear when the clock struck six. Weekends found her streets still pretty empty, and the few services, shops, and restaurants that were there were closed. While it was quieter, for Karen it was too quiet. She felt isolated.

The fact that she had shopped unwisely, or rather that she had not shopped at all, became clear as she visited friends living in other parts of the city. They seemed to live in neighborhoods that were truly alive and engaging. People actually lived there. They could buy milk.

Find a Place Where Somebody Knows Your Name

In many countries the glorious ritual of pub-sitting is pursued with something akin to religious zeal. People regularly drop in to their local tavern or cafe and leisurely nurse a pint of beer or cup of coffee while making conversation with others from the neighborhood. We see it here, but in slightly altered forms. True, we still have our Norms, Cliffs, and Carlas, but nowadays beer and beer nuts are quickly giving way to mocha frappuccino and vanilla biscotti. The watering hole of choice these days is likely to be a cafe in a book-store or a coffee bar on the corner where you share a couch with a Monica, a Rachel, or a Chandler.

Look for cafes, restaurants, coffee shops, delis—places that are people friendly and encourage locals to linger, sit, watch, and talk. Seek places that you find inviting, places you would feel comfortable spending time in, and people you would enjoy being with. As the *Cheers* theme lamented, "Sometimes you want to go where everybody knows your name." Or if you require a little more anonymity, at least a place where you see a familiar face or two.

Look for a Community

Finding that you are part of a larger community becomes an important source of inner strength and resilience. You feel a sense of personal centeredness and of being connected to others. Unlike a neighborhood, a community is harder to recognize. It is the intangible glue that makes you feel you belong to a neighborhood or, for that matter, an entire city. Communities are made up of invisible but meaningful relationships between people.

What you *can* see however, and what you should look for, is the *potential* for community. Then it is up to you to put in the time and effort to become a member of that community. The best way to determine whether a community has potential is to talk to people who live in the neighborhood.

Ask about neighborhood churches or synagogues, charity organizations, civic groups, block associations, co-op or condo associations, parents associations, or any other form of participation where people come together. These are the building blocks that ultimately turn a neighborhood into a community.

Live Near a Park

There is a magnificent park about three blocks from where we live, and frankly I cannot imagine living in the city without it. When our kids were smaller we took them to the playground. Now we stroll, sit, picnic, bump into people, and just hang out there. As luck would have it, the park borders a river, and we can watch the sailboats go nowhere in particular. The commotion of the city is, for a short while at least, forgotten.

A park becomes a natural oasis. You need to spend some time in a place that isn't concrete, doesn't make a lot of noise, and is roughly the color green. It does not have to be large. All you need is some expanse of grass and trees, a relatively uncluttered vista, and some respite from the noise of traffic and the hustle and bustle all around you.

Live Near Somewhere You Can Sweat

If staying in shape is not one of your priorities, it should be. Stress takes its toll on your body and the wear and tear over time can leave you vulnerable to a wide variety of maladies and disorders. Keeping fit enhances your ability to resist and defeat the omnipresent city germs and viruses.

But a gym or a health club is more than a place where you care for your body. It's also a place where you feel connected to others around you and to the neighborhood in which you live. Like a local pub or coffee shop, it is a setting that can be used to meet your social and emotional needs. It puts you next to your neighbors in ways that are comfortable and relaxed. You feel you are a part of something; you feel you belong there. A gym or health club can do as much for your psyche as it does for your abs. Maybe more.

Never Underestimate Convenience

One indisputable advantage of living in a big city is the availability and convenience of stores and services. Take advantage of this.

After you have found a place that meets most of your primary criteria for a livable neighborhood, do a "convenience check." Imagine that you will be living largely within a radius of a dozen or so blocks from your home. Walk around the neighborhood. Start by tracing small "convenience circles" around where you might live and begin widening these circles. Make a note of what kinds of shops and services you find as you go along. Is there a supermarket nearby? A fresh fruit market? A dry cleaner? A bank branch? A movie theater? A gas station? A bookstore? A shoe repair shop? And of course, a video store and a Chinese restaurant.

If you use your car a lot, and do not have a garage or parking spot, ask about the ease and availability of parking in your neighborhood. Some city folk spend an incredible amount of time every day trying to find a parking place near their home.

Also inquire about buses, subways, and streetcars. Where are the major stops? How far are these stops from where you live? How frequent is the service? Find out how to get to those places you most often need to be or want to visit. Ask, "Can you get here from there?"

Make It a Safe Place to Live

Safety has always been a concern of those who live in a big city. While we are currently witnessing a decrease in city crime, what you really should worry about are the chances of something happening to you in *your* corner of the city. Specifically, you want to know:

- Are the streets in your neighborhood safe?
- Can you walk around the neighborhood at night?
- Are there many burglaries and robberies in the area?
- Is it safe for kids to play outdoors?

Ask locals how safe they feel living in their neighborhood. Then check with the local police precinct and find out what types of crime occur in this neighborhood and how the crime rate compares to other parts of the city. Most bigger cities keep rather detailed statistics on types of crime and where they occur.

Also find out from neighbors and from the police about the specific crime history of the house or apartment you are considering moving into. Some places seem to be more attractive targets for would-be burglers. Don't be naive about crime. Bad things can happen and do happen in big cities. They also can happen anyplace you live.

But Don't Become a Crime Nut

When I first came to New York, I was a crime nut. New to the city and totally frightened by horror stories of crime and pillage, I was paralyzed by fear. I believed that walking these streets would surely result in my demise.

I distinctly remember my first job interview in the city. As my taxi approached the street and building where my meeting was to take place, I could feel my heart racing as I dashed from the cab into the lobby of an upscale East Side office building. I was certain that I would be robbed, assaulted, or worse. Needless to say, I survived.

Be careful not to *over*exaggerate the safety factor. Yes, safety *is* important. However, many people are so traumatized by crime that they overreact to the potential dangers of the city and wind up living either in a sterile part of town or in an overpriced, triple-door-manned city fortress. There's a big difference between a healthy sense of concern and immobilizing fear. Don't go cuckoo.

FINDING THE RIGHT SPACE

As Miss America, my goal is to bring peace to the entire world and then to get my own apartment.

—JAY LENO

In Tom Wolfe's popular eighties novel, *The Bonfire of the Vanities*, the central character remarks that once you have lived in a place that costs $2.6 million, it is impossible to live in one that costs $1 million. Those of us accustomed to living more modestly might find that discomfort somewhat easier to bear. But Wolfe makes a good point: It is never easy going backward, no matter how far forward you have come.

For many, living in the city means going backward. This is particularly true when it comes to the space where you will live. Urban realities give you fewer options and fewer choices. Your living space in a big city ultimately becomes a compromise.

For most of us, our dwellings look like something between a Seinfeldian one-bedroom (or less) and a Cosby-type brownstone (from his *old* series), or even a Murphy Brown townhouse. But unless your uncle left you a pile of money, or your company is about to go public, you can be reasonably certain that the place you live in and the space you occupy will fall a tad short of your ideal.

Where you live is one of the most important factors determining just how stressful your life in the city will be. No other single feature of life in the big city is as important as your home. Your place should be an island of comfort, your personal sanctuary in the city that insulates you from the chaos that lurks just outside your door. You have to choose wisely and compromise very carefully.

Start Slowly but Learn Quickly

I remember when Beth and I, newly married, looked for a place to live in the city. We fell in love with the very first place the agent showed us. We were ready to sign, pay, and move. "Not so fast!" something within us warned. So we asked the Realtor to show us a second place. Thank God we hadn't taken the first! This time it was *true* love. Then that "something within us" acted up again. So we saw a third place. Much better than the first or second. This definitely felt like the real thing, but maybe the next one might be even better. So we abandoned the third and looked at a fourth. Big mistake. As it turned out, all the places we saw after the third seemed far less desirable, and the ones we had liked were now taken. We ended up looking at many more places before we found another we really liked.

I've always suspected that the Boy Scouts were thinking of real estate when they chose "Be Prepared" as their motto. When you are considering a new place to live, naturally, you would like a little while to think about your options. Well, you do have a little while, a *very* little while. The irony is that you probably have more time to choose bathroom tissue or table napkins than the place where you will live. When it comes to real estate there's almost always a sense of urgency and near panic. Usually, there is an agent or a Realtor breathing down your neck warning you that the place won't be on the market long and that there is a long line of willing buyers or renters, and unless you commit within the next three minutes this place is history. And sometimes they are right. Places in a big city can move fast. You have to have a pretty good idea of what you are looking for. You have to be ready to act.

Finding a home in a big city means recognizing there is a learning curve, and then climbing that curve as quickly as possible. Sometimes, of course, you may have to pass up something good to know that it was good. However, the more information you have, the more people you've talked to, and the more places you have seen, the more you will be ahead of the game.

Don't Scrimp

I know, I know: Less is more. Or certainly can be. But when it comes to where you live, less can be *less*. Spend the bucks. Either find a place you do like or take the place where you live now and turn it into an environment that you enjoy. Get, or create, the best available home for yourself given the realities of your budget. Don't let the cost kill you. You do not need to get into serious debt. Do not sell your body on the street. But do get the best you can realistically afford. If necessary, trade off. Get a cheaper car. Buy fewer shoes. Pack your own lunch.

Think Smaller

Frankly, even if you are willing to spend more money, you still may have to get used to the idea of living in a smaller space. This is especially true if you are coming from a home outside the city. Living in the city usually means settling for fewer rooms or smaller rooms or both. Kiss good-bye any fantasies of a mega square footage floor plan. We're talking smaller here. Much smaller.

However, this need not signal the end of civilized life as we know it. Smaller spaces can be wonderfully charming and welcoming, and can make the perfect sanctuary. In fact, living in a smaller place will help you simplify your life. It gets you to recognize that you may not need all that "stuff." It makes you re-evaluate which possessions are important in your life and which are not, and hopefully helps you to unload those things that you really don't need to keep.

Find a Place Where You Can Linger Outdoors

One of the nice things about country or even suburban living is just how easy it is to have access to the outdoors. Non-urbanites are able to idle in their yards, fuss with a petunia, or swing on the porch while the sun sets slowly on the horizon. Alas, horizons in the city are hard to come by, as is time outside.

There are times at the end of the day and on the weekend when you do not want to be inside just yet. You want to be home but you still want to linger outdoors. Having a place with a front or backyard can be wonderful. If that is unrealistic, try to find a place with a terrace, even if it is a very small terrace. The smallest bit of outdoor space can allow you to stay out and extend the day. We have neither a yard nor a terrace, but we are fortunate enough to have some space on our roof that allows us to tinker, barbecue, plant, and just sit, relax, and be outside. It makes an incredible difference in the way we experience our lives in the city.

Listen before You Lease

A quick question. Before you plunked down that hefty down payment or rent deposit, just how much time did you spend in your home-to-be? An hour? Half an hour? Twenty minutes? And did you notice just how noisy the place was?

Noise is rarely our major concern when we choose a home, but it should be a serious concern if you live in the city. While you should expect some noise living in a big city, you do not want to discover that noise is making your life even more stressful than it already is. You want to sleep at night, and you want to be able to hear your child's first words or the sound of your own telephone ringing. Never be in the position where you find yourself uttering the following:

- "Gee, when we came through with the agent the place seemed so quiet. I never imagined we would be living next to Mr. and Mrs. Party-Time."
- "Isn't there a law that says you can't make that much noise before 7 A.M.?"
- "I never knew you could actually make walls out of paper."
- "Maybe the death penalty for noise offenders is not such a bad idea."

Listen for unusually noisy neighbors. Listen to the traffic. Remember young children can be heard as well as seen. Look out for neighborhood businesses with noisy ventilating systems or air conditioners. See the place at different times of the day. Many clubs, cafes, and restaurants can be silent all day but become unbelievably noisy in the early hours of the morning. Ask the people around where you are considering living about their experiences with noise. Look, ask, and *listen*.

Seek the Light

Light becomes very important when you live in a large city simply because there is not enough of it. Cities can be relatively sunless. It may be the size and number of the buildings blocking your rays or it may be because you spend 95 percent of your time indoors. Sadly, many offices, department stores, and even restaurants are relatively windowless. In winter, cities in northern climes can become even bleaker places.

People need light. We know that sun and light can affect our moods. Living in a place that has too little light can depress the heck out of us. We feel happier and more positive when we live in a place that is bright and airy. Look at the number, size, and exposure of available windows. Look to see if there are any skylights. Turn off any artificial lighting and see how much natural light there is in each room. If possible, come back at a different time of day and see how the lighting has changed.

Get a Room with a View

What you see when you look out of your windows has an enormous impact on the way you feel. Looking out over a deserted alley or facing a large apartment building can be depressing. A pleasing view, on the other hand, can lower your pulse rate and restore a sense of calm and serenity. Few in the city can boast of overlooking a river or a park. Some might claim a skyline. Most of the rest of us look out on far less impressive vistas. Your view doesn't have to be particularly grand. A pretty yard, an interesting building facade, or even a single tree can make a big difference.

Charm Yourself

At least a little. By "charm" I mean you should try to find some feature or aspect of your space that delights you or touches you in some way. It could be an attractive piece of molding on the ceiling, a wooden floor, an especially high ceiling, the curve of a window, or an arch of an entranceway. A fireplace, especially one that works, is a real asset, if you can find one. Nothing connotes coziness, warmth, and serenity more than the idea of sitting in front of a crackling fire. As a bonus you can barbecue chicken in your living room in the middle of winter.

MAKING YOUR HOME A HAVEN

In fact there was but one thing wrong with the Babbitt house; it was not a home.

—SINCLAIR LEWIS, *Babbitt*

Whenever I visit people's homes in the city I am surprised at the very different feelings each can evoke. Not every place feels like a home, and not every place feels like a haven from the stress of the city. Maybe the Feng Shui is faulty, or maybe it's a lack of decorating know-how. There are certain houses and apartments that always feel warm and welcoming and that put you at complete ease. Your breathing slows, your stress level drops, and you realize that the tension in your body is now a fraction of what it was before you crossed that threshold. And then there are those places that offend the senses and seem to add to your stress level.

I remember when, after my parents died, my sister and I decided to rent out their house for a few years. We carefully screened a list of prospective renters and soon found a lovely couple who liked the place and agreed to move in. They had one request: Could they re-decorate? Sure, why not? Though I loved my home growing up, I always found my parents' taste a little too conservative. From time to time I would catch myself mentally redecorating the various rooms. So with mixed feelings, but largely hopeful expectations, I awaited this "before-and-after" makeover.

And what a job they did. They transformed the entire house. Their choices in furnishings and accessories were tasteful, well matched, decorator perfect. The place was truly worthy of a maga-zine spread. My mother's reaction, I suspect, would have been shock, followed by a fall to the floor. My reaction? I hated it.

Yes, I understand that there is much sentiment attached to the place you grow up in, and any change is difficult. But I found the house's new incarnation uninviting and cold. For me this new house was not a place where one would ever feel cozy and wel-comed. The furniture was severe and imposing. The seating was hard, and the lighting was harsh. The open surfaces and counters seemed sterile, devoid of any human touch. Though the aesthetics were impeccable, the house felt lifeless and devoid of any soul.

There is no simple formula that turns a place into a warm and welcoming abode. However, there are common elements of struc-ture and design that can contribute to a greater sense of calm and tranquillity. Your choice of lighting, furnishings, accessories, color, and texture can all play a role in enhancing the warmth and emo-tional texture of your space.

But achieving a sense of peace and calm involves more than having the right interior decorator. It also comes from the small personal touches and additions that create a relaxing mood. They may be photographs, a pet, a plant, a childhood collection, any number of things. It may also be something as simple yet important as the sound of quiet, or a pest-free kitchen that makes your life more tranquil.

Flirt with Urban Minimalism

The idea of living in a room with nothing but a lamp and a rug leaves me cold. Yet the minimalist model can be an inspiration for us all.

One of the common pitfalls of living in a big city is overfurnishing. We may have moved to the city from larger quarters and brought with us all the furnishings that comfortably filled our previous space. But, what worked nicely in a three-bedroom house usually requires a shoehorn to fit into a city-sized, two-bedroom or smaller apartment. You do not want to be crowded by your chair or your sofa. Your home and its furnishings ought not be a major source of stress in your life.

Brighten Up

If you do not have access to natural light, make artificial lighting work for you. Imaginative lighting can create a sense of enhanced space and dramatically change the feeling of a room, leaving you in a better mood. However, not all lighting works equally well. While I am sure that a naked 300-watter in the middle of your ceiling will give you all the light you need to read the newspaper, I also suspect that after a couple of weeks of living in this room you may find yourself more than a little depressed and looking for a rope and a stool.

One way of creating warmth and interest is to use multiple lamps of lower wattage placed at different places in a room. This provides a warmer glow, especially if you can find the right lampshades. A halogen lamp is great for providing loads of ambient light, but sometimes the brightness and whiteness can be cold and monotonous. Decorative lighting can highlight a painting, bookshelf, or corner of a room. A dimmer switch can change the mood of a room dramatically, and candles can add an air of romance and tranquillity.

De-Stress with Color

Color can make a room larger or smaller, formal or casual, inviting or distant. It can affect the way you feel and the ways others feel when they spend time with you. Psychologists have determined that certain colors have different psychological effects on us. Here are some of their observations that can help to guide your choices:

THE COLOR	THE PSYCHOLOGICAL EFFECT
Soft Pink	Peaceful, restful; stronger shades suggest Double-Bubble
Black	Sophisticated; often used to impress others
Red	Arouses, stimulates the appetite
Earth Tones	Relaxes; makes one feel mellow
Soft Blues, Greens	Peaceful, nonstressful

In some rooms you may go for peace and tranquillity. In others you may want intensity and excitement. Lighter colors can create a feeling of openness and greater space. More intense colors can work well in smaller rooms but if you spend a lot of time in that room, pick a color you can live with. And remember there are no hard-and-fast rules when it comes to color. If you like it, go with it. To hell with fashion. However, whatever your color choice, try it out on a part of your wall first. Those microscopic paint chips can look terrific in the paint store and dreadful on your wall.

Become an Urban Gardener

If you are lucky enough to have a few square yards of outdoors, put them to use. Even a few square feet of space on a patio, a window ledge, or a rooftop can give you enough space to plant some flowers or put out some houseplants. A small herb garden in the kitchen can make your home feel more welcoming.

Watch out, however, for high-maintenance greenery. Look for plucky plants, plants that are survivors and can hold their own against the pollution, lack of sun, and the all-around inclemency of city life. Below are some city-tested recommendations:

TEN "FOOLPROOF" CITY HOUSEPLANTS

1. Aspidistra   Aka the cast-iron plant. Loves the city. Has urban attitude.

2. Sansevieria   Aka the snake plant. Needs little light. Doesn't give a damn.

3. Cactus   A legendary urban survivor. It will probably outlive you.

4.	Rubber Plant	Can do very nicely in cool, even dim interiors.
5.	Philodendron	Can still make it even with little light and little water.
6.	Dracaena	Aka the corn plant. Terrific in a hot, dry apartment.
7.	Spider Plant	It will take just about everything you give it.
8.	Bromeliads	Need a misting now and then but seem to flourish with neglect.
9.	Nephthytis	A true friend of the city. Is forgiving of neglect.
10.	Dumb cane	Does just fine with little light and little moisture.

Reflect

Mirrors can do more than ensure that your makeup is applied correctly or that you don't slice your throat shaving. They can help add a very different dimension to the space you inhabit, and they are relatively cheap and easy to install. Personally I was never crazy about too many mirrors. With a heavy hand, you can easily turn your place into something one visits at the fun house. Yet carefully placed mirrors, in a narrow hallway or above a mantel, can produce a feeling of openness and lightness. Mirrors can be used not only to make smaller spaces appear larger, but also to bring additional sunlight into a normally drab room. Mirrors can also enhance a view or at times provide you with a view that would not otherwise be possible. Smaller mirrors strategically placed can add to the visual interest of a space. Also, mirrors can make a large, not particularly attractive piece of construction or furniture smaller and less obvious. Experiment.

It's the Little Things

One of my favorite places in our home is our hallway. Hanging on one wall is an assortment of our family's photographs. Proudly displayed on another wall is our son's and daughter's "art." In fact, just about wherever you look you can find little things that remind us of times and pleasures past. It is these "little things" that add feelings of warmth and connectedness to our home. Some suggestions:

- Books and photographs can add great warmth and comfort to a home. Neatly aligned in a bookcase or openly displayed on a table or cabinet, they introduce a sense of stability and coziness. Photographs are a powerful way of connecting you to where you live.
- Collections of various sorts—art, pottery, weavings, miniature elephants—whatever. It could be little Caroline's rocking horse from Sotheby's, that Barbie doll you've kept all these years, or that saxophone that you played, briefly, in high school. Touches of whimsy. Splashes of wit.
- Music can change our moods dramatically. It helps us to wind down, relax, and regroup. Consider installing some kind of music system or extension speakers in those rooms where you spend a lot of your time.
- Fresh flowers can bring a ray of sunshine into a home. Their presence can create a sense of serenity and simple beauty. Their smell can be transporting.

Minimize the Sound and the Fury

A quiet city is a contradiction in terms. The city is rarely quiet. There is a constant din created by car horns, car alarms, police sirens, fire truck sirens, screeching brakes, garbage trucks, never-ending construction, and road repair. And that's just outside.

Indoors it can be worse. Boisterous party-loving neighbors, successful musicians and singers, unsuccessful musicians and singers, or simply an overly aggressive twist of the volume control can make your life a living hell. Complaining may or may not remedy the problem. Consider the following ways to make your space a little quieter:

- **Soundproof.** Windows are often the weakest link when it comes to noise from the outside. Even with the windows shut, there can be a lot of sound that still comes through. Consider installing double-pane windows. Heavy drapes or shutters can add to the soundproofing and even make the room look better. Carpets, rugs, wall hangings, pictures, bookcases, and bookshelves will all help absorb excess noise. Recently I read an obituary of a well-known city writer who was a fanatic about quiet when he wrote. He covered his room entirely in sheets of cork. It helped. You may not have to go this far.

- **Mask It.** The secret of masking is finding a more tolerable noise and making it the one you hear. Most of us experience masking in the summers when the soothing hum of the air conditioner drowns out just about everything else. A sound generator can mask and calm. Newer models can reproduce just about any sound you might find soothing—a waterfall, a rain forest, or the chirping of crickets in a meadow. A relaxing tape or CD can work just as well.

- **Block It.** That Metallica groupie upstairs or a deafening sanitation truck outside may call for stronger measures. There are times when earplugs may be an answer. A light sleeper myself, there has been many a time when I have turned to my earplugs for relief.

But Don't Become Noise Traumatized

I have had more than one patient in therapy who was noise traumatized. In each case the process starts fairly sensibly. First you hear a noise coming from your neighbor's place. It is loud and distressing. You try to wait it out, but it continues. You cajole, complain, threaten, and then it seems to go away. But by now you are a changed person. You are now a noise fanatic.

You are obsessed with the possibility of hearing any noise. Continually vigilant, you listen all the time. You notice when your neighbor comes and goes, when he turns anything sonic on or off. You are ready to do battle at the mere hint of a decibel. It consumes you, even though—and this is the looney part—the actual noise has never returned to its original distressing volume or anywhere near it. It is now the *idea* of noise, rather than the noise itself, that becomes the problem. Catch yourself and self-medicate before you get to that stage.

Own a Pet

There is abundant evidence showing that pets can indeed reduce our stress and serve as important sources of comfort. The presence of a pet in the room can put us at ease, evoke pleasant nurturing feelings of tenderness within us, and give us a companion. Pets can lower our blood pressure, make us feel more relaxed, and distract us from our own worries and concerns. And since they don't complain, have opinions we dislike, or know how to operate the TV remote, they trigger less conflict and friction than others with whom we may live. As a bonus, they can even take care of your roach and rodent problems.

Our family has two cats, Emma and Skittles. They are house cats, meaning they have never gone shopping or seen a play. And other than Skittles's one possible suicide attempt (she fell two floors), I would have to say that they are quite happy living in the city.

Conventional wisdom suggests that animals and cities do not mix. It says that having a pet in the city is not a great idea. A goldfish or a chinchilla might work, but anything larger is a big mistake.

Forget conventional wisdom. If you are predisposed to having a pet, get one. I still remember the words of one city friend who told me the best thing she ever did was get a dog. And indeed, if you take the time and make the effort, having a pet in the city can succeed wonderfully. Not only will the animal be happy, its owner will find having one is a marvelous antidote to the stresses of the city.

Bless This House

Introducing a spiritual dimension into your home can become an important way of giving it a special feel. Traditional holidays, of course, provide well-defined ways of expressing ritual and observance. Family customs and repeated family events in the home all contribute a sense of warmth and belonging. They include commonly observed religious practices, such as saying a prayer before or after a meal or putting up a wreath or tree at Christmastime. It is common for many families to have religious objects in the house as well. For instance, in the Jewish religion it is common to place a small printed blessing or mezuza at the entrance to one's home.

Other approaches may be totally secular. It could be lighting candles at a special dinner or having a welcoming message above the front door. It can be as simple as eating dinner with the family at the same time each night, toasting everyone's health at a meal, or singing songs at a family get-together. It could be telling your kids a bedtime story every night. Whatever the ritual, whatever the symbolism, whatever the ceremony, a home, to truly be a haven, needs a soul. Give yours one.

5

Controlling the Chaos

A car is useless in New York, essential everywhere else. The same with good manners.

—MIGNON MCLAUGHLIN

*A*while back, my daughter, then in the third grade, brought home a math problem she needed some help with.

Sally has an errand to do in the city. Later this afternoon she plans on driving downtown and returning a dress to a department store.

At what time will Sally get back home, if:

- she leaves her house at 3:30 p.m.;
- she estimates it will take about 20 minutes to drive to the store;
- she plans on staying in the store about 25 minutes and then going right home.

There are two answers of course: the textbook answer, and the real one. Assuming Sally lived in a large city, the actual time taken would be longer than she planned. Sally needs some help with *her* math.

Come on Sally, wake up and smell the espresso! You *know* that you will never make it to the store in twenty minutes. By three-thirty, the early rush hour is *already* in full gear. Coming home you will be smack-dab in the middle of it. You'll be lucky to make that trip in anything under forty-five minutes. Twenty-five minutes in the store? Where have you been shopping all these years? Burger King? If you figure the time it takes getting to and on an elevator, battling the crowds, finding a clerk who isn't busy, getting served even in a reasonable length of time, completing the paperwork . . . You're looking at an hour—minimum. You will be a fortunate woman if you see your front door again before six o'clock.

One might think that coming and going in a large city would be a piece of cake. After all, living in the city spares you the long commute of your suburban friends. Everything is really pretty close. And when you get to where you're going, there are generally more than enough stores, services, and places to meet all your needs. The problem is, however, you are not alone.

Big cities are big cities because they are filled with people. And whenever you have too many people all wanting to do the same thing at the same time, you have stress. Your particular headache may come from bumper-to-bumper traffic, overcrowded stores, constant rushing, or endless waiting. Whatever the source of your navigational woes and congestive misery, this chapter will show you how to relieve much of the pain.

AVOIDING THE HERD

That restaurant is so crowded nobody goes there anymore.

—YOGI BERRA

Whenever I think about traffic and crowding in a big city, I always come up with the same two images. The first is a piece of documentary-style footage showing hundreds of people walking on Fifth Avenue in Manhattan at the peak of rush hour. The film is shot with a powerful telephoto lens that compresses four city blocks into one. People look as if they are but millimeters apart. The accompanying music is Philip Glass: atonal, driven, frenzied. The feeling I get is one of tension and pressure, and for some inexplicable reason I have this intense craving for sardines.

The second image comes from the film *Falling Down*, where Michael Douglas's character, finding himself trapped by a horrific traffic jam on an L.A. freeway, goes totally berserk. He has had it with the stress, strain, and the general incivility of modern life. Frustrated and angry, he embarks on a rampage of hostility and destruction.

The fact is, no one really has a problem driving on a deserted road or walking on an empty sidewalk. And no one has a problem with short lines or shopping in an uncrowded store. The truly toxic element in getting around the city is the traffic and crowding. And because there are so many of us in a big city, there is almost *always* traffic and crowding. Here's what to do.

Create a Waiting/Delay List

While some of your waiting is unavoidable, much of it *can* be avoided. What you want to minimize is any waiting that is habitual and predictable. The first step is becoming aware of those times when you find yourself waiting. Take a minute or two to review a typical week, and mentally circle the instances when you find yourself having to wait for something, or when your progress is delayed. Come up with your "Waiting/Delay List." My list looked like this:

CIRCUMSTANCE	WAITING/DELAY
Waiting for the subway every workday	0–10 minutes
Missing a subway because of overcrowding	5–10
Waiting in line for coffee every morning before work	5–10
Waiting at the post office	0–30
Stuck in slow-moving traffic	10–30
Waiting at the dry cleaners	0–10
Waiting for movie tickets	0–25
Waiting for delivery of a purchase or repairman	30–still waiting

The good news is I have now eliminated, or at least reduced, my waiting time for most of the items on my list. Here are some ways you can clear up *your* list.

Master the Art of "Off-Peaking"

Cities have their own daily rhythms of activity. These are the times of day when it seems as if just about everyone simultaneously decides to go to the bank, eat their lunch, buy their groceries, and rent a video. Stay in sync with this rhythm and you will find that you have lots of company. The trick, or skill rather, is to get *out* of sync by mastering the contrarian arts of off-peaking and time-shifting. Simply put, do what you have to do when few others are doing it. Here are some suggestions.

- Avoid doing your banking on Fridays. Also avoid lunchtime. The beginning, middle, and last day of the month are also busier times at banks. Use the ATMs whenever possible. Bank by mail. It is amazing the kinds of banking transactions you can now do on your computer. In most cases your bank will give you the software free.
- Unless you can't wait, schedule your doctor and dentist appointments just after lunch or mid- to late mornings. Friday afternoons can be a busy time for any doctor or dentist doing in-office surgical procedures, as people prefer the idea of having the weekend to recover.
- Mondays can be very busy days for gyms and health clubs. Following a weekend of sloth and gluttony, and re-motivated by guilt, everyone hits the StairMaster. The wait for a particular piece of equipment can tax the most patient set of abs. Later in the week the numbers drop off. Lunchtime is more crowded but not as bad as after five-thirty. Mornings and afternoons can be a great time to work out if your schedule will allow it. I try to get to the gym in mid-afternoon when it's only me, the cleaning lady, and these three guys who look like Arnold.
- Restaurants can be packed at prime times. If you are going out for lunch or dinner, try to eat either a little later or a little earlier than the mob. The service is better and the atmosphere more re-

laxed. And you get a better table. In an area where there is theater, you'll find that you can usually get a table at eight p.m., just after the pre-theater diners are asking for their checks.

- If a movie theater is in your neighborhood, buy your movie tickets earlier in the day when you are doing other errands. Then get to the theater about five minutes before the movie is to start. Assuming you need only one or two seats together, you can be pretty well assured you will find them. Most movie theaters now have computerized ticket sales and know when the theater is full. Some now even assign you specific seats when you buy your tickets.

- If the movie is a blockbuster and/or you need more than two seats together, get to the theater just after the previous showing has finished. A movie theater can be a pleasant place to chat, listen to your favorite tape, or simply relax for a few minutes between movies.

- In most larger cities many things can be done at night, after normal closing times. There are all-night drugstores, supermarkets, bookstores, video stores, and just about everything else you might need.

Follow the Fifteen-Minute Rule

In terms of square miles, cities are really pretty small. When there is no traffic you can traverse most cities relatively quickly. This can result in a distorted perception of how long it takes to get somewhere. In big cities, the amount of time it actually takes to get somewhere is always greater than the amount of time you think you need. You miscalculate, and you find yourself rushing.

You may also make the mistake of assuming that once you get to an address, you are there. You forget that meeting someone on the twenty-fourth floor of a busy office building means waiting for an elevator, getting to the right floor, and finding the right office. That takes time. By failing to factor in all of these variables you find yourself feeling harried, often late, and always frustrated.

One good way to avoid this stress is simply to add fifteen minutes to the time you estimate it takes to get someplace. If you get there early, use this downtime to catch up on other things, or simply relax. If you are arriving much too early, cut back. If you find that the fifteen-minute estimate isn't enough, crank it up to twenty minutes. Experiment. You will find that you hurry a lot less and feel a lot less harried.

Go on Foot

Whenever I have to get from here to there in the city and the distance is not too great, I go by foot. I realize that for many this may seem a somewhat radical notion. There are, however, many times when walking is the least stressful, and at times most efficient, way of navigating the city. The fact is, most of our trips around the city are pretty short. More than half of all trips in the city are less than two miles. In New York City the average crosstown speed of a car is now an abysmal 5.2 miles per hour. I can walk almost that fast. In other major cities, the speed may be higher, but not by much. The average walker could easily cover a mile in fifteen minutes. Even if the trip were somewhat longer, we could still walk.

Walking places does take some getting used to, especially when larger distances are involved. But you will rarely be bored, and there are health and psychological bonuses. Remember, too, that you do not have to mess with traffic and the cost and hassle of finding a parking space. And you do not have to worry whether your radio or air bags will still be there when you get back.

Go Public

When I don't walk I use the public transit system for most longer-distance trips in the city. For the most part it is fast, and relatively painless. In most cities, using public transportation, at least some of the time, can make your life a lot easier. But many of us reject this option. Taking the bus, trolley, or subway seems like such a pain and taking our car seems infinitely easier. It is this anticipation of discomfort that is the greatest obstacle to using mass transit.

The best way to overcome this is to get your feet wet. Leave your car at home for two weeks and take mass transit. Master the system at least to the point where you can comfortably navigate around the city.

Reading your newspaper on a bus is far less stressful than worrying about what the other lunatic drivers are going to do next or waiting for the gridlock to clear. If you get a seat, sit back, relax, and think about the money you are saving.

The subway system, if your city has one, can be incredibly efficient. Yes, it can be crowded, but going underground can be the quickest way to get from here to there. There are times when I go home from the office by cab, yet the time I save compared to taking the subway is minimal. At rush hour the subway is the faster alternative by far. And it is not the horrible place some people make them out to be.

Take a Taxi

There are times when being transported in a car may be the option of choice. Inclement weather, taking your aging relatives to bingo, attending a gala event clad in your finest raiments—all may warrant calling or hailing a cab. Taxis may seem like an expensive alternative to owning a car, but if you do the math you may be surprised at how the yearly cost for infrequent rides looks more reasonable when compared to the cost (parking, gas) of using your car. And if you do not own a car, the saving is substantial. Cabs are simple. You get in, argue with the driver for a few minutes, and you get out.

Let Your Fingers Do the Walking

When you live in a big city, you quickly learn that the telephone and fax machine can be some of your best friends. By dialing the right combinations of digits and pressing the right buttons, you can save copious amounts of time, avoid lanes of traffic, and completely bypass those oppressive crowds. And why not take advantage of one of the idiosyncrasies of the service industry: A salesperson or clerk will generally pick up a ringing phone even though there is a long line of people in front of them who have taken the trouble to come down in person to get the same thing you are calling for. (Note, however, that this principle does not apply if the organization is part of the government or is a publicly owned utility. In those instances your call will never be answered, or you will be put permanently on hold.)

So spend that quarter. Call for just about anything you need. Here are some useful phone/fax options to help you avoid congestive hassle.

- Buy your movie tickets over the phone. Then simply pick up the tickets when you arrive at the theater. There may be a small service charge, but the savings in terms of time and energy can be substantial. In most big cities you can also dial a number to find the location and starting times of most films currently playing.

- Many big-city supermarkets will allow you to phone or fax in your order. They will also deliver them to your door for a reasonable fee. See if your local supermarket offers a catalog with most of their products listed and priced.

- Phone or fax in your prescriptions. Better yet, have your doctor call it in. Why spend twenty minutes looking at hair-care products and suntan lotions while the druggist fills your prescription?

- Video shopping in the store at peak times can be a discouraging process, with most of the good stuff already taken. You find yourself going home with *Police Academy 9* or some other Siskel & Ebert thumbs-downer. If you can't get to the video store right away, call them up and ask them to hold your selection for you, or even better, have them deliver it to your door.

Work the Web

The newest and perhaps most intriguing way to avoid lines and searching for a parking spot is to go online. These days the Internet offers buying access to most goods and services. With a few well-placed pecks on your keyboard and clicks of your mouse, you can summon up any one of thousands of available websites. There have been times when I have done my banking, purchased plane tickets, made reservations at hotels, and bought books online, all without waiting or being ignored by a single clerk.

An efficient way of using your computer to help you access services and products is to get a hold of a list of "The Very Best Websites" or "The Top 50 Websites" published in computer magazines usually at the beginning of each new year. There are also website directories that can be used like telephone books to get the proper addresses.

Catalog (Cautiously)

Catalog shopping can save you much of the hassle of crowded stores and long lines. They can be especially useful at peak shopping periods such as Christmas. Just about everything and anything can be found in one catalog or another. But there is a downside. Catalogs take up space and they can become habit-forming. Limit your catalogs to the bare minimum. Pick the one, two, or maybe three that you *really* find useful. Cancel all the rest.

Join the Club

Subscriptions and memberships can be a good way to consolidate the amount of time you spend on a habitual endeavor and to avoid repetitive, minor errands. The most obvious example is subscribing to a magazine. Sure, you could go out and buy it at the newsstand every week, but long ago you realized that it was more convenient to subscribe. Buying ahead can shorten your wait.

Get Off the Beaten Track

Not only do people decide to do everything at exactly the same time, but they all do it in the same places. What's popular tends to be what's crowded. But don't make the mistake of equating "popular" with "the best," or the most value for your dollar. Smaller, out-of-the-way, lesser-known restaurants, cafes, shops, and services abound in a big city. These may be places that are on their way up, or even on their way down, or simply never got noticed. Whatever the reason, you'll rarely have to wait in line.

In our neighborhood we have a dazzling array of places to choose from. Yet the "hot" local places are impossible to get into. Luckily, there are shops and services that are almost never full because they are slightly out of the way. They might be located on a side street, or on the second floor. Whatever the reason, they never became trendy. I am sure our favorite Mexican restaurant wouldn't be as empty as it always is were it better located. Bad for them, good for us.

WINNING THE WAITING GAME

And next?

Dr. Crane, on line two, we have someone who's having a problem with delayed gratification.

Well, he's just gonna have to wait!

—From an episode of *Frasier*

One of the advantages of city life is the accessibility of everything. It's all there. The disadvantage is you may have to wait for it. Hurry and wait. It could be the city's motto. It has been estimated that we spend up to a tenth of our lives just waiting. We wait for movie tickets, laundry tickets, ATMs, bank clerks, store clerks, grocery lines, traffic jams, elevators, doctors, buses, delivery men, that table in a restaurant, and for that ninny on the other end of the telephone to take us off hold.

There will be times when, no matter what you do, you're "just gonna have to wait." Though you have diligently mastered the art of off-peaking and have time-shifted most of your waking hours, you still find yourself stuck in traffic or waiting in line at the Kwikie-Mart. *How* you wait, however, and the amount of distress you generate, is something you *can* control. Winning the waiting game means knowing how to play.

Maybe It's a Personality Thing?

Not everyone is cut out for waiting. Maybe your personality type is not suited to it. Too bad, because you are just going to have to wait anyway. But blaming your impatience on your emotional makeup ("Hey, that's just the way I am!") can reduce some of the guilt. Listed below are some of the prime characteristics of poor waiters. See how many describe you.

THE WAITING SCALE

Place a checkmark in the boxes that apply to you.

1. I have trouble doing nothing for even a short time. ☐
2. I become very impatient when I have to wait. ☐
3. I get easily angered when others are late for appointments. ☐
4. I drum my fingers, fidget, pace, or tap my feet a lot. ☐
5. When driving I frequently change traffic lanes. ☐

---

6. I am easily distracted. ☐
7. I often start things, but do not finish them. ☐
8. I change channels or radio stations frequently. ☐
9. I have trouble reading the directions before jumping in. ☐
10. I feel restless without a lot of action in my life. ☐
11. I have a hard time reading a book from beginning to end. ☐
12. I am having trouble sustaining enough attention
to finish this list. ☐

Your score: _____

Checking off five or more boxes would suggest that waiting may not be your psychological strong point. But even though you may be a poor waiter, all is not lost. Even the poorest of waiters can learn how to wait.

Expect to Have to Wait

The biggest mistake we make when it comes to waiting is perceiving a wait as an unusual and unnecessary occurrence. Rather than viewing it as something expected and predictable, we determine the waiting to be an anomaly, an exception to the rule. So we head off for that doctor or dentist appointment for three p.m. and expect that at the stroke of three the receptionist will emerge to usher us into the doctor's office. Yeah, right.

Similarly, on finding ourselves sandwiched and immobilized in a lane of traffic, we exclaim, naively: "I can't believe this!" Well, believe it. And believe it when you find yourself lining up with hordes of others at a ticket counter or waiting for a table in a restaurant. And *learn* from it.

Start with the more realistic expectation: "Since I have waited for just about everything and anybody many times before, it would be clever of me to expect to wait again." Expect traffic, expect crowds, expect congestion, and expect to wait. Turn your expectations around. Be surprised when you *don't* wait.

Amuse Yourself

Sometimes hassles and inconveniences are really opportunities in disguise. Waiting, too, has its upside. You can make your waiting time productive, entertaining, or at least pleasant.

Personally, my favorite thing to do when I find myself having to wait is to daydream. I relish the opportunity to mentally veg and let my mind wander. Of course there are other more socially redeeming things you can do when you find yourself waiting. When you find yourself a prisoner of the supermarket checkout line, pass up that copy of *The National Enquirer* for something with a little more meat. Rather than learning about alien babies, or what Carolyn Bessette Kennedy's hair color is these days, read something a little more stimulating. Have some interesting reading material in your pocket or purse whenever you go out. It could be an amusing little paperback or an article you cut out of the paper last week but haven't found the time to read.

Some people carry a Walkman or CD player with them, which are turned on at even a hint of a possible wait. If you are caught in traffic in your car, having a good selection of music can soothe your wait. These days the selection of books on tape is incredibly wide.

You can pick and choose from a list that includes most popular novels, poetry, and collections of short stories. You can even learn another language if you are so inclined.

Waiting time is a good time to catch up on some of the organizing and planning that still has to be done. It could be used to put together a shopping list, update your To Do list, or jot down some notes to yourself about an upcoming event or trip. Just be sure to have a pen or pencil and a piece of paper with you.

Practice Some Auto-Relaxation

Try this simple technique while caught sitting in traffic or even stopped for a red light.

STEP ONE: Inhale fully through your nostrils, expanding your belly. At the same time squeeze the steering wheel firmly with both hands. Hold that breath, continue to squeeze for about four or five seconds and then . . .

STEP TWO: Exhale fully through your slightly parted lips while releasing your grip (don't let go of the wheel). As you exhale, imagine a wave of relaxation flowing from the top of your head, down through your body, all the way to your toes.

Repeat this process whenever the opportunity arises. You will find it will help you relax fairly quickly and slow any buildup of muscle tension in your body.

Use the "Forever" Technique

Exaggeration has a way of putting things in perspective. Bringing a smile to your lips won't shorten the line or lessen traffic, but it can make the waiting less distressing.

When you find yourself having to wait, mentally exaggerate the wait to the point of ridiculousness. For example, suppose you are waiting in line at the department of motor vehicles in an attempt to renew your license. By the length of the line and its speed of progress you reckon that this process will take forever. That's the operative thought you want to work with: forever. Now imagine that you have taken a number from the dispenser. It is a very high number. Your number is 70098. They are currently serving number 4. The years pass. You are still in line. Your children finish college. They come to visit you, bringing you food and snacks. You've developed close relationships with those in front of and behind you. There is talk of having reunions. . . .

Do the Opposite

There is an episode of *Seinfeld* where George, realizing that his normal instincts have gotten him nowhere, decides that he would be much better off by doing the exact opposite of what his instincts suggest. He may not be entirely off base here. There are times when the best way to get where you want to go is to go in the exact opposite direction.

For instance, sometimes it's only by trying to stay awake that you can finally fall asleep at night. The same principle holds for overcoming the need to hurry. Try some of these exercises. Odd as they may sound, they really can help you reduce your level of impatience and help you become a better waiter.

- At the supermarket or bank, choose the *longest* line to stand in.
- If you find yourself caught in the "wrong" lane in traffic, stay in that lane.
- Force yourself to listen to or watch a really boring presentation or television program.
- When the elevator, bus, or subway comes, wait for the next one.

While in these usually hellish situations, observe yourself experiencing all of your normal discomfort. Now focus on the thoughts producing this distress. Begin turning your feelings around by doing the following: 1. Relax your body by taking deep, slow breaths. 2. When you notice your low frustration tolerance coming to the surface, combat it with some coping self-talk:

"I don't like this, but I can deal with it."
"I do not want to be upset and angered by stuff like this."
"This is hardly a major disaster. I can cope."

And indeed you can.

6
Getting Organized

I hate housework! You make the beds, you do the dishes—and six months later you have to start all over again.

—JOAN RIVERS

I have fond memories of disorganization. I smile whenever I recall my father's unique organizational style back when I was growing up. He was an electrician by trade, and our home was his warehouse. He would fill every nook and cranny of our house, garage, and car with all sorts of electrical paraphernalia—wire, fuse boxes, ladders, fluorescent bulbs, more wire, screws, wall plates, and more wire. I was always delighted when I would open a drawer, almost any drawer, and discover a wealth of wonderful electrical odds and ends, which with a little ingenuity and some assembly, would become my next project.

Our garage was a particularly good place for my father to store his materials. Space for a car or even a bicycle was out of the question. It was quite literally filled from top to bottom with his stuff. There was so much stuff that the one small door that remained accessible could barely be pushed open. One day, however, a pile of something fell behind the door and so even that would not open.

The garage became a filled and sealed tomb, and for the next ten years, until my parents died and the house was to be sold, was never opened again.

Hopefully your home is not as disorganized as ours was, but if you live in a big city, your organizational skills and resources will definitely be stretched to the limit. Unfortunately, when it comes to inefficient organization and management, the city can be unforgiving. Lapses are poorly tolerated. Knowing how to effectively manage and organize your life in the city becomes a necessity.

CLEARING AWAY THE CLUTTER

I did not have three thousand pairs of shoes;
I had one thousand and sixty.

—IMELDA MARCOS

If you live in the suburbs or the country, clutter can be perceived as a charming oversight. In the city it can easily become a debilitating disease. Too much stuff can overwhelm you. Eventually, you'll feel like you're drowning in that clutter. You need a life jacket.

The reasons why you find yourself up to your neck in clutter are not that mysterious. First, you probably do not have enough room. In a big city you have less space to begin with, and still fewer places to store things. Secondly, your life is now much busier and you have less time to figure out what to do with everything you own. Eliminating clutter seems less of a priority. Until, of course, you realize that you have absolutely no more room for anything else—not that latest copy of *Newsweek*, not a paper clip, not anything—and that you would surely die of embarrassment if the wrong people unexpectedly came to visit.

The first step in managing clutter comes from truly believing that your life would be immeasurably improved if you owned fewer things, if you had a little more room, and if you could find the TV remote or the mates to your socks hidden somewhere in your bedroom.

You, however, may be one of the handful of people whose home does not look like *Pee-Wee's Playhouse*. The word *clutter* may elicit no response on your polygraph. You may, incredibly, be clutter-free. Take this short quiz to see if you should just skip to the next chapter.

ARE YOU "ORGANIZATIONALLY CHALLENGED"?

For each item below, simply <u>circle</u> either <u>T</u>rue or <u>F</u>alse.

1. When friends come to visit, they ask if your place has recently been vandalized. **T** or **F**
2. You distinctly remember owning a pet, but cannot seem to recall the last time you saw her. **T** or **F**
3. Although you think your friends are kidding when they call you a slob, a mess, and a skuzzball, they do not appear to be smiling when they do so. **T** or **F**
4. When you offer your place to friends from out of town, they always turn you down, and on one occasion they indicated that they would prefer to stay at the homeless shelter. **T** or **F**
5. If you had to find something in your place in a real hurry, and let's say your life depended on it, rather than spending the time looking, you decide you would be better off making funeral arrangements. **T** or **F**

Answering true to any of these items is not a good sign.

Find Your Favorite Clutter Excuse

Unfortunately, finding the time and motivation to get rid of our unnecessary possessions is very difficult. Given a high "in-out ratio" (more items coming in than going out), the inevitable result is clutter and the sinking feeling that you are slowly being devoured by your life space. When cornered, we would, of course, cleverly defend this self-defeating behavior. Here are some of my favorite excuses.

The Ten Most Common Reasons to Never Throw Something Out

1 I might need it someday.

2 My aunt gave it to me for my eleventh birthday.

3 Someone might pay big bucks for this.

4 I'm sure I'll find the matching one eventually.

5 It still works.

6 It can be fixed.

7 If I just lose ten pounds I'll fit into this.

8 It will be an antique one day.

9 Our kids will need it when they have kids.

10 I really plan on reading it.

Stop Kidding Yourself

Fooling yourself is much easier than you think. Some part of us really believes that we *will* clean out that closet, *donate* those old sweaters to charity, and *hand down* all our hand-me-downs. We also believe that we *will* eventually use much of the stuff we haven't used in eons, that anything with even a whiff of sentimentality must be kept no matter what, and if something is worth a few dollars, it is worth keeping—forever. Alas, we are mistaken.

Just Start

I have always liked that Nike bit of philosophic exhortation, "Just Do It!" Yet as a psychologist I recognized that "just doing it" for most of us is not going to do it. My T-shirt would read a bit more conservatively. It would say: "Just Start!"

In your heart you know that once you get rid of most of that unwanted stuff you will feel much better. Stop delaying the effort and postponing the decision. Just start.

Salami Slice

It would be terrific if you could put in one or two hours and get your life organized and be done with it. Let's face it, it took a lifetime to collect these fabulous possessions, and it may take more time than you would like to eliminate or reorganize all this stuff.

One way of jump-starting yourself is to "salami-slice." Rather than seeing all the clutter in your life as one massive pile, see it as a succession of tasks that can be accomplished piece by piece, slice by slice. Start with some clutter that you see as relatively self-contained. Once you have dealt with this bit of clutter move on to the next, and so on until your entire home is as neat as Martha Stewart's sock drawer.

Make It Worth Your While

As the late psychologist Abraham Maslow pointed out, much of our lives operates within a hierarchy of motivators. If you are dying of thirst in a desert, a glass of water is what you desire most. Once your thirst is quenched, you probably want something to eat. And then, of course, theater tickets.

Sometimes your level of internal motivation won't get you where you want to go. You need some external motivation. You can do this by either rewarding yourself for doing something, or giving yourself a penalty for not doing it. Create your own "motivational ladder." Simply come up with a list of things that could motivate you to get the job done and then rank them in order of their importance to you. For example:

- Treat myself to a minivacation.
- Buy myself something big, something I've been dying to get but have denied myself.
- Treat myself to a great meal or even a dessert.
- Go to the movies, a play, or do something fun.
- Buy myself a small present that I would enjoy.

Work with Shame

We find that our home is at its organizational best about seven minutes before a large number of guests are due to arrive. In fact the cleaning-up process leading up to that first doorbell ring is filled with energy and determination. Of course it is. We would surely die if people saw our place the way it usually looks.

Shame can be a powerful motivator. It used to be that the power of guilt was just as strong and just as effective. But not these days. We feel a little bit guilty, but not enough to get us to plug in a vacuum cleaner. No, better to work with shame. Set a date when you will invite a number of people over to your place whose respect, opinion, and approval you desperately need. This time make your low self-esteem work *for* you.

Schedule It

When we schedule things, they have a better chance of getting done. We generally show up at our dentist and doctor appointments, our business meetings, and at most other engagements that we purposefully schedule. The same tactic can work when it comes to getting things done around the house. Commit to a definite time and write it down in your calendar, daily planner, or whatever you use to keep track of your life.

Be Ruthless

Simplifying your life space takes grit. Your attitude as you approach the task should be "I am sick and tired of this and I am not going to take it anymore!" You may find my approach a bit too merciless, but be clear, we are dealing with an evil force. Give no ground. Take no prisoners. Here are some therapeutic questions that will help you increase your grit.

- "Do I really want to spend the next twenty years living with this?"
- "If my place were on fire and I could save only half the things I own, would this particular item be one of them?"

- "Would the quality of my life be seriously diminished if I didn't own this?"

Triage

A big obstacle to getting rid of things is the seeming lack of a middle-ground solution. The two choices seem obvious: "Should I keep it, or should I get rid of it?" This dichotomous, yes-or-no decision can be too hard to make. One trick I have found useful in overcoming this decisional avoidance is to use something I call "The Triage Method of Clutter Control." Here's how it works:

STEP ONE: Create three categories: 1. "Definitely Keep"
2. "Definitely Throw Out"
3. "I'm Not Sure"

STEP TWO: Throw out or give away everything in categories two and three.

The penalty of having made a mistake is far outweighed by the benefits of unloading all your junk and clutter. Do it and don't look back.

Lose the Paper Trail

Those who have made the study of clutter their life's work tell us that *paper* is the major villain. Get rid of your unneeded, unwanted paper and you are three-quarters of the way to solving your clutter problem. Here's how.

- **Junk Your Junk Mail.** When the junk mail comes, throw it out immediately. Do not open it. Do not become curious or intrigued.

Keep a trash can near your mailbox or your front door. Realize that no matter how much mail you receive from Ed McMahon or Dick Clark, it will never make you rich. When a catalog comes, peruse it, use it, or lose it. Get yourself taken off mailing lists. Call the Better Business Bureau or look under Direct Mail Associations listed in your telephone book. They will tell you the number in your area to call to get you removed from many of the more annoying lists.

- **Read It Now.** Most of those articles you want to save are better read at the time you see it. If you do not, it is highly likely that you will never read that article again. Either read it, make it your "waiting-in-line" material, or chuck it.

- **File It.** There are items, however, you want to hang on to. You may want to keep an article, recipe, travel brochure, toaster warranty, instruction manual, medical record, or that receipt you will need at tax time. Cut out only the part you need and immediately put it into a file appropriately labeled and include it in your filing system.

Get a Clutter Buddy

Whenever my wife and I decide to de-clutter, we both find that we each have marvelous ideas for clearing out the *other* person's side of the room. We seem to be a lot more creative and certainly more ruthless disposing of the possessions of others. Use this psychological fact of life to your advantage. Invite your spouse or a friend to guide you as to what stuff should go. Of course, you will happily return the favor.

But Don't Go Overboard

Personally, I cannot imagine living in a place without *some* clutter. Those *Architectural Digest*–type rooms and homes leave me aesthetically inspired but also emotionally detached. It takes too much effort and anxiety to maintain the clutterless home. When people really live in their homes there is evidence of everyday living, past and present—scattered possessions, yesterday's newspaper left on a chair, unwashed dishes in the kitchen, an uncapped tube of toothpaste in the bathroom, and half-read books and magazines scattered about.

The goal is not magazine-perfect rooms, minimalist chic, or a spartan life space devoid of all but the bare necessities. Some degree of intended or accidental clutter and disorganization can be satisfying and emotionally comforting. Rather, it is the unwanted and distressing clutter and disorder that needs to be eliminated. Don't defoliate. Just prune.

MANAGING YOUR TIME

There's never enough time to do all the nothing you want.
—BILL WATTERSON

One might think—mistakenly, of course—that living in a big city means having more free time. After all, compared to your rural and suburban friends, you are on a vacation. Your home is probably smaller so you dust less, clean less, repair less, and repaint less. You spend much less time clearing gutters, uncluttering garages, painting fences, repaving driveways, and cleaning the swimming pool.

Your lawn, if you have one, is certain to be smaller, so you mow less, rake less, and water less. You do not own a weed whacker or a snowblower. Your daily commute is probably shorter, so you spend less time in trains and cars. You seem to be ahead of the game. Yet somehow all of this does not translate into more spare time. In fact, you find you have less, and you are in good company. Most city dwellers share the same wish: "Just give me two more hours in the day."

The numbers tell it all. In any one day:

- we sleep for seven hours and twenty-five minutes.
- we work for seven and a half hours (the minimum for most of us).
- we groom for forty-nine minutes.
- we do household chores for sixty-six minutes.
- child and pet care takes twenty-five minutes.
- grocery shopping takes sixteen minutes.
- preparing meals takes thirty-four minutes.
- we are in transit for fifty-one minutes.
- we watch television or videos for 154 minutes.
- sex . . . (well, *you* make your own estimate).

Since there are twenty-four hours in each day, there appears to be very little time for anything else. City time is a different kind of time. City hours are shorter, and city minutes are, well, mere seconds. You find yourself with more to do, and less time to do it. Your life becomes more unpredictable, and it is the city, and not you, that sets your agenda. Unless you begin to manage your time carefully, you quickly learn that the city will manage it for you. And that's *real* stress.

Divide and Conquer

Take a piece of paper and list the most common ways you spend your time. List the kinds of things you do regularly and routinely. Then sort them into one of two groups that reflect the level of your distaste for them. Here are the ways my preferences break down.

THINGS I WANT TO SPEND MORE TIME ON	LESS TIME ON
Time with family	Late office hours
Time with friends	Office paperwork
Staying in shape	Cleaning the house
Reading and learning	Laundry
Keeping up professionally	Being with people I do not enjoy
Traveling	Watching television
Playing tennis	Attending events I do not enjoy
Cooking	Commuting
Learning Spanish	
Making pottery	

Armed with your list, you are now in a position to allocate different strategies to meet the different activities. Those items on the left side of your page are to be encouraged, extended, savored, and enjoyed. Those on the right, you want to minimize, eliminate, delegate, and generally avoid when possible.

Use the "Will Do" Method

Knowing your priorities is a major first step. Now you can create a road map and organize your day. Most of us simply do not plan our days, so the city pushes us around. Try using this simple "will do" method.

Get a small notebook, calendar, set of index cards, electronic organizer, or whatever your own personal preference is. But make it something you can easily carry with you. On the top of the left-hand page (or back of a card) write the words *To Do*. On the right-hand page draw three columns. Title them:

WILL DO	WHEN & WHERE?	WHAT HAPPENED?

Toward the end of your day, give yourself ten minutes to think about the next day and update your planner. On your <u>To Do</u> page or card, jot down all the things you should do or would like to do the next day. From this bigger list, enter in the <u>Will Do</u> column of your planner only those things that have high priority or importance in your life. These are the tasks that must be taken care of because if they're not, you will feel stress.

The list can be long or short. However, enter only those items you commit to doing. Make a pact with yourself: "If I write it down, I do it." This is not a "Things I would like to do" list, but "Things I will do." For example:

WILL DO	WHEN & WHERE?	WHAT HAPPENED?
Call for plane tickets	10:30, my office	Called. Got them.
Write letter to Donna	2:30, at lunch	Done. Mailed.

If, for whatever reason, a task didn't get done, and it is still important, put it back on the list. If you chronically leave tasks undone, shorten your list. The secret of this simple system is that it minimizes procrastination and avoidance and maximizes follow-through.

Buy the Time

Many of us operate under a work ethic that says, "Never pay anyone to do anything you can do yourself." This is a mistake. Often, making your life simpler and less stressful and giving you more time to do the things you like to do mean paying someone else to do the things you do not enjoy and/or do not have the time for. Hire someone, and spend the bucks. The payoff can be greater than you think.

Am I being cavalier about your money? Not at all. I realize that you do not have a lot of extra cash lying around. However, there are times when hiring someone else is clearly the smartest option. Gone are the days when it was only the very rich who hired someone else to help them.

Here are some questions to help you decide whether hiring someone makes sense for you.

- What chores do you absolutely hate to do?
- What chores constantly provoke a battle between you and your spouse, or you and your roommate?
- What chores do you merely dislike doing?
- What chores do you not do very well?
- What chores do you not mind doing, but really aren't worth your time and effort?

Here are some of the chores and services you might want to pay someone else to do for you.

- Regularly clean your whole house or apartment (kitchen, bathroom(s), dishes . . .)
- Do your laundry.

- Pick up your groceries.
- Wash your windows or clean your rugs.
- Repaint or refinish your walls, furniture, or floors.
- Take care of your yard or garden.
- Take care of your pet when you are away.
- Buy and wrap that gift you need.
- Get tickets for you.
- Wait in line for you.

Realistically assess your financial ability to hire someone to do some of the items on your list. Remember also that the emotional relief and the extra time gained in many cases are well worth the money.

And of course it doesn't have to be a licensed professional. It could be a student or that friend of a friend. In a big city, you find lots of people "between opportunities" who would be quite willing to help you out. Look at lampposts, local billboards, or the newspaper for names and numbers. And always ask for references.

Strive for Deliverance

One of the advantages of living in a big city is the incredibly large number of errands that can be accomplished without leaving your home. Almost anything can be delivered to your door—groceries, videos, laundry, liquor. Take advantage of any and all free services available to you.

Minimize Interruptions

Much of your time can be consumed by small interruptions that distract you from the tasks you must do and lengthen the time it normally takes to complete them. You'd be surprised to discover how much control you can have over these distractions.

Let your telephone answering machine take all your calls. Then you won't have to hear that pitch about why you should switch your long-distance carrier again. Even better, install caller ID. That way you will know who is calling and decide whether you want the machine to pick up or if you really want to speak to that person at that moment. And even if you do not have all this electronic gadgetry, not answering the phone every time it rings will hardly handicap your chances of having a good life. When people want you, they find you.

If you are at home, move to a room where you know you will have the most privacy. If you are at work, close your office door, if you have one. Most important, curb those interruptions that you manufacture. Once you begin a project, no matter how small, finish it before going on to something new. And remember, you do not need a break every two minutes.

Curb Your Electronic Dillydallying

Our fifteen-year-old son once observed, "Have you ever noticed how much longer the days are when you don't watch TV?" The same can be said for the other forms of electronic entertainment. I'd be the first to admit that the TV, the personal computer, the Internet, and Nintendo are marvelous inventions. However, all can easily become black holes, sucking in all your free time and energy and providing very little in return.

Try to cut back on the time you spend watching TV. Never just randomly channel surf, sticking with the "least-objectionable" program. Rarely watch a television program when it is first broadcast. Use your VCR. Tape and collect the programs you like, and watch them in a block, at a time you choose. Don't watch television at other times, and never watch more than a few hours of television in any one week. When your recorded tapes are approaching a number that is not humanly possible to watch in one whole day of dedicated TV viewing, start winnowing. Begin recording over an existing tape rather than adding another to your growing collection.

Limit your hours with an online service or the Internet by pre-scheduling when you will log on. Keep a very simple log taped to the monitor and check off when you used it and for how long. Never sign on for more than a few hours in any week. Give most of your computer games away.

Do something else. Read a book. Go to the gym. Make soup. Make love. Go to bed earlier.

SPENDING LESS

Save a little money each month and at the end of the year you'll be surprised by how little you have.

—ERNEST HASKINS

There's no doubt about it, living in a big city can be very expensive. Simple economic principles dictate that where there is a high demand and limited supply, everything is going to cost more. Housing (renting or owning), clothing, transportation, education, food, and entertainment can cost a bundle. So how can anyone afford to live there?

Well, some can't. Many of my patients complain that they cannot make it in the city on their current salaries. Some of them make a lot of money. They work in lucrative fields that pay generous salaries. Annual bonuses push those figures even higher. Yet they are struggling. They spend money very quickly. At the end of the year they find there is not a whole lot left in the bank. I also see other people with far smaller incomes who live in the city. Their lifestyles are more modest, yet curiously they seem less troubled with the stresses of money and finance.

The fact is, above a certain income level, the amount of money you make does not appear to be strongly correlated with the level of your financial woes. A large paycheck may not guarantee fiscal relief. In the final analysis, managing money in the city comes down to managing your priorities. What is important to you, or what you think is important to you, will determine whether you spend a little or a lot. Whatever the level of fiscal distress you experience may be, it comes largely from the difference between what you can afford to spend and what you actually do spend. Figure out how to reduce that differential and you will find that you sleep a little better at night.

Know Where Your Money Goes

When it comes to spending our money, we can be incredibly casual and careless. The first step in reducing your fiscal stress is acquiring fiscal awareness. You need to know where your money is going. I am not suggesting that you record the whereabouts of every dollar you spend, but I am suggesting that you keep a record of where most of your money goes.

To accomplish this, you can go low-tech or high-tech. Going the paper-and-pencil route, keep a record of every expenditure you make over twenty-five dollars. Then in a separate column jot down the reasons why you can justify this outlay. If nothing else, this simple approach will force you to be more aware of your spending habits and make that extra purchase a tad more painful than it normally would be. This way you'll be able to see where your money goes and you'll be on your way to establishing control over it rather than the other way around.

Computerizing your expenditures with some of the financial software currently available can make your budgeting efforts easier. By entering the expenditures on your computer you can quickly get a summary of where your money is going. With a little practice you can come up with fancy charts and graphs documenting your financial smarts.

Be Pound Wise

It is our major expenditures that determine whether we feel a little stress or financial panic. You will have to cut coupons till your scissors get dull to recoup the big bucks you spent for that home theater system, or the mega-outlay for that new car, or the serious dollars you will need to send your kid to that private nursery school. That's a lot of breakfast cereal.

We are often "pound foolish" when it comes to our spending. We can easily rationalize major spending without much discomfort. And sometimes the rationale has a certain appeal. Some of the more common convincers include:

- "You only live once!"
- "If it's for the kids, I get the best there is."
- "I don't do this every day."
- "How many times do I turn twenty (thirty, forty, fifty . . .)?"
- "I'm getting an income tax refund."
- "I'm getting a big bonus soon."

Yes, sometimes this thinking makes sense. Often it does not.

Look, But Don't Buy

Temptation can run high in a big city. You have to learn to resist. Just because there is something you might like to buy does not mean you have to buy it. I like to bake, but I actually eat very little of what I make. I find the process and the sense of enjoyment sufficiently satisfying. Similarly, when it comes to shopping, there is a big difference between *looking* and actually *buying*. There is a satisfaction you can get by shopping for something, looking at windows, sales counters and sales catalogs. Indulge your desire to look; curb your impulse to buy.

Some questions you might ask yourself before you open your wallet.

- Do I really need this?
- How many of these do I own already?
- Can I live a happy life without this?
- Will it truly add to the quality of my life?

For many, if not most of the things we buy, the answers to the above are No, Enough, Yes, and No.

Buy It Used

A big city is the ideal place to pick up just about anything second-hand. Flea markets, thrift shops, and used-everything stores abound. Furniture, clothing, appliances, books, CDs, and most anything else can be picked up at a fraction of its original price. Take a pass on that thong. Everything else is fair game.

Consider a Roommate

We tend to think of a roommate as a rite of passage—something one has while away at college, or maybe for a short period after school until we get on our feet and get our own place. The notion of a grown man or woman having a roommate seems a bit unusual. Unless, of course, you live in a very expensive city.

These days more and more city dwellers have decided to find someone to split the rent with. The old rule of thumb that one's rent or housing costs should not be greater than 25 percent of their income is a joke if you live in a city. City dwellers have found that mailing their paychecks directly to their landlord leaves little room for the other necessities of living. And even if your rent is not strangling you, it's still nice to have more money left over at the end of the month to spend on other necessities.

Many people are surprised to discover that they actually like living with a roommate. Many prefer it. Having a friendly face around the house can be very appealing. The trick, of course, is not finding a roommate but finding the *right* roommate. In most cities, and certainly in the larger ones, there are services dedicated to doing just that. As there is an abundance of people looking for roommates, you have the luxury of being a bit choosy. Interview as many as possible before you finally decide. And once you have found someone, it is a good idea to have two phone lines and even a cleaning service just to make the shared life a little less rocky.

Spend Less on Your Car

Transportation can be one of your bigger expenditures, no matter where you live. Keeping a car in the city can cost you an arm and a leg. Parking is expensive, gas is more expensive, and insurance premiums are usually higher. Having your car towed or repaired in a big city can be a sobering experience. If you can't do without your car, at least use it less. It has been estimated that you can save up to a hundred dollars a month if you leave your car at home and use public transportation. If you're going to buy a car, consider buying a used one. If you absolutely must have that new-car smell, buy last year's model just after the new models come out.

Eat Well, Not Fancy

Eating out is an intrinsic part of urban living. And you can do it without breaking the bank. Many new visitors to the city wind up going to one of the more expensive restaurants in town. They suffer near–cardiac arrest when the check comes. "The food was good," they remark, "but not *that* good!" Every city has a slew of great places to eat, and not all of them are that expensive. You just have to explore a little.

The first thing to do is to get your hands on an up-to-date restaurant guide. Better yet, find one that lists only those great places in town that are also inexpensive. Once a year you can take your mother to La Maison D'Excesse for her birthday.

Find That Entertainment Bargain

It would be a shame to live in a big city and not take advantage of many of the cultural and entertainment opportunities that abound. The trick is not to spend a fortune while doing so. Remembering that you spent seventy dollars for a ticket can be a distracting experience as you watch the performance. Yet with a little time and a few queries you can quickly find ways of getting to see shows, performances, exhibits, and movies at reduced prices. Subscriptions are certainly one way to save some money. So are the half-price tickets or "two-fers" that many productions promote once a show has lost some of its novelty. Smaller productions can be significantly less expensive and are often surprisingly good.

Every big city offers an array of free cultural events, sometimes during lunch hours, but often in the evenings and on weekends. Concerts, operas, readings, plays, and productions of various sorts are all there. Just read the newspapers. And check with the cultural events office at City Hall. They will send you the information you're looking for.

Sometimes Shop with the Big Boys

I have always been a strong believer in shopping locally and patronizing your neighborhood vendors, especially when it comes to routine, day-in, day-out kinds of purchases. It can cost a little more, but the added expense is more than compensated for by the convenience and the sense of community you feel.

There are, however, times when big bucks are at stake. Purchasing a big-ticket item like a new car or a major appliance can run into major dollars. At times like these, the larger chains and out-of-town megastores are your option of choice. Size, of course, is no guarantee of a cheaper price. You still have to comparison shop and hunt for that big bargain.

Be Wary of Buying in Bulk

The concept of bulk shopping has everything going for it. After all, it can be much cheaper. So why not buy the items you need in huge amounts? If you live in a big city, you should ask yourself one or two questions before you start loading up your car.

- Where will I put these four hundred rolls of toilet paper? Under the bed? Behind the television?
- Do I really want this carton of hair cream to be passed on to my children and their children?
- If this two-gallon jug of spaghetti sauce goes bad before it is half eaten, have I still saved a lot of money?
- Do I really know what a jar of this stuff sells for elsewhere? Am I sure I'm paying less?

Sometimes a bargain just isn't a bargain.

7

Staying Healthy
in the City

To me the outdoors is what you must pass through in order to get
from your apartment into a taxicab.

—FRAN LEBOWITZ

If cities came with a warning label, it might read: "Living here
may not be the best thing for your health." When we conjure up
an image of a typical city dweller, we picture a pale complexion
and a neglected body. We think of urbanites as poorly nourished,
insufficiently rested, and under-exercised, weakened by too much
time spent in crowded elevators, stuffy offices, and polluted streets.

Sure, there are some city folk who fit this description. But there
are many more who do not. In fact, this stereotype is way off the
mark. The truth is, you can probably find more physically fit people
in big cities than in the suburbs or in the country. Urbanites as a
group tend to be very health conscious. And certainly body conscious. We want to look better and feel better.

Are your health and fitness patterns good enough to prepare you
for the grueling demands of city life? Take this short pop quiz to
find out how your lifestyle rates.

Your Urban Health and Fitness Profile

For each of the five items below, simply circle the answer that best describes your current lifestyle.

1. For me, a "balanced meal" means
   (a) including at least one item from each of the major food groups in every meal.
   (b) eating less red meat and eating more vegetables, fruits, and grains.
   (c) downing a hot dog and soda while standing in a moving subway car and not falling on top of my food.

2. For me, a "good night's sleep" means
   (a) eight or nine hours of uninterrupted sleep.
   (b) six or seven hours of uninterrupted sleep.
   (c) doing anything with my eyes closed for more than four hours.

3. For me, "working out" means
   (a) working up a sweat at my health club.
   (b) jogging two or three miles a day.
   (c) carrying my laptop from my office to my car.

4. I have found that the secret to effective meal planning is
   (a) cooking more than one meal at a time.
   (b) owning several very good, low-fat, low-calorie cookbooks.
   (c) having an excellent selection of take-out menus taped to my fridge.

5. The *best* way to lose weight is to
  (a) eat less and exercise more.
  (b) join a well-regarded weight-loss program.
  (c) smoke a lot, and cram as much stress into your day as possible.

Scoring:

Answering (c) for any question suggests that the rest of this chapter is required reading. The rest of you might find it useful as well.

EATING RIGHT

Never eat more food at one sitting than you can lift.

—MISS PIGGY

City dwellers think about food a lot. For many of them food is a passion. Unfortunately, passions can lead to overkill and abuse. Eating in the city can turn into a nutritional disaster. It is feast or famine, and food either gets a lot of attention or becomes an afterthought. Eating patterns in a big city are at best *inconsistent*. More often than not, you'll find yourself tailoring meals to fit a hectic schedule. Chances are, you'll end up either grabbing a slice of pizza on the corner or sitting down to a two-hour lunch at La Maison D'Excesse.

In addition, we urbanites like to eat out a lot. We eat in restaurants more often than our suburban or rural counterparts. We also like to eat in, but spend less time preparing meals, preferring to order in food or to pick something up on the way home. But whether we dine in, or dine out, our eating habits could probably benefit from some fine-tuning.

Stop Feeding Your Stress

Many of us are emotional eaters. We eat whenever we are anxious, upset, nervous, or depressed. Unfortunately, the foods that tend to make us feel good are usually the foods that are not so good for us. Chocolate, ice cream, pizza, cake, donuts, and cookies make us feel terrific. Unfortunately the feeling never lasts. It stays with us for about twelve seconds, or until the guilt and anxiety return and we feel the need to inhale another pint of Ben & Jerry's.

Label Your Feelings

When you feel the urge to open the refrigerator door, you may be experiencing some form of discomfort other than real hunger. The first step in breaking the cycle is becoming aware of exactly what you are feeling, and labeling that feeling. Ask yourself, "Am I really hungry or am I feeling stressed?" If it is truly hunger, eat. Otherwise label your feelings: "I'm upset." "I'm nervous." "I'm a wreck!" Then do not eat. Do something else.

Surprisingly, simply by breaking the stress-eating connection for even a moment can give you a different perspective and an increased level of motivation that can sustain you until you come up with an alternative to filling your mouth.

Feed Your Brain

In the last few years there has been a growing interest in the connection between food and mood. Specifically, people have been looking at the relationship between our brain chemistry and the kinds of foods we consume. The outcome has provided us with some natural ways of reducing the amount of distress in our lives by monitoring what we put on our plates.

If you find that you are feeling blue, or that your emotions go up and down like a yo-yo, you may be experiencing the effects of the foods you are eating. One way of helping you discover if your mood swings are food-related is to keep a food-mood diary for two or three weeks. Simply keep a record of any negative moods you may be feeling and when and what you ate that preceded that mood. If food is your problem, a pattern should become apparent in a relatively short period of time. You may find that you need to pay more attention to your brain's chemistry and feed it what it needs, thereby avoiding a shrink or a dose of Paxil.

Make sure that every meal has some complex carbohydrates. Pasta, cereals, potatoes, and brown rice can make us feel better emotionally. Foods rich in carbohydrates contain the amino acid tryptophan, which can increase the levels of serotonin in the brain and make us feel better in a way similar to the way some antidepressant medications work.

Reduce your intake of sweetened foods. Sugary foods like soda and candy can make you feel better temporarily, but in the long run, you will feel worse. Increase the amount of foods rich in B vitamins. Eat more whole grains, fish, chicken, bananas, legumes, and dark green, leafy veggies. B vitamins and other nutrients become serotonin in the brain.

Make any changes slowly and don't expect overnight results. Many of these biochemical changes take time before you notice any improvement in your mood. And if negativity in your mood continues, it is always a good idea to check things out with your doctor.

Boost Your Mood

If you are anxious, nervous, or stressed out, a quick dietary fix can offer relief. Here are some specific suggestions for foods that can boost your mood and help alleviate some of that urban stress.

- a turkey sandwich on whole wheat
- a handful of mixed nuts
- a bowl of whole-grain cereal with a sliced banana
- a spinach salad
- a roast beef sandwich
- a bowl of fruit salad
- a piece of chocolate (one piece!)
- a cup of coffee (one!)

Eat Your Breakfast

Your mother was right. One of the simplest things you can do to enhance your body's ability to cope with the stress of the city is to not skip meals, especially breakfast. Because eating habits can be so erratic in a big city, it is important to get off on the right nutritional foot. When you wake up in the morning, as many as eleven or twelve hours have passed since you last ate. You need to refuel. You may feel fine skipping breakfast, but studies show that people who habitually skip this meal often report feelings of fatigue later in the day and many times overeat at later meals.

What should you eat for breakfast? Avoid sugar and the usual high-fat villains—ham, bacon, sausages. A cup of coffee or two won't hurt but try not to go overboard with caffeine. Including a low-fat, high-fiber, multigrain cereal with some low-fat milk in your morning routine will get you off to a good start. I like to mix my cereals, combining a few frosted flakes with some All-Bran and some puffed wheat. I also like oatmeal. It's fast, especially if you use the instant kind, and it sticks to your ribs. Recent studies have shown that oatmeal provides you with a sustained, long-lasting release of energy—longer, in fact, than any other kind of breakfast cereal.

Graze

Spread out your eating evenly throughout the day. Avoid huge meals that load you with calories and leave you feeling ready for a siesta. Have a snack sometime during mid-morning, then a light lunch, another snack later in the afternoon (a piece of fruit is good), and a *moderate* dinner. A snack later in the evening (try some air-popped popcorn) should avert any hunger pangs. In fact, for most people the simplest way to lose weight is to eat more in the first half of the day than you do in the last half. Then you have time to burn off many of those earlier calories.

Master Fast Food 101

Fast food flourishes everywhere, but in the city you find more adults than kids in the take-out lines. To be fair, more healthier items are appearing on fast-food menus, but you need a map to navigate the nutritional potholes. Here are some fast-food pointers.

- Go with turkey breast or lean roast beef instead of salami, ham, and cheese.
- Avoid the chef's salad. It sounds terrifically healthy, but isn't.
- Tuna is great. Add a lot of mayo, though, and it becomes a mistake.
- Have a hamburger instead of a cheeseburger.
- Never order a "large" anything.
- Eat at a salad bar. Selectively.
- Eat only half of your french fries.
- Have a slice of pizza without any meat toppings.
- Take the skin off your order of roasted chicken.
- Try having a "lite" yogurt and a piece of fruit for lunch.

Cure "Menu Weakness"

Let's say you are tired of the same old Chinese, Mexican, Thai, Vietnamese, Italian, and Hungarian fare and are ready for some solid, generic food. You head for the local true-blue diner with the best of dietary intentions. The waitress hands you a menu. Now, faced with a list of enticing options, your common sense flies right out the window. You find yourself overcome by a wave of "menu weakness."

This clinical condition, though not fatal, can be harmful to your health. Menu weakness strikes when we order things we later regret ordering, like french-fried onion rings, or that hunk of steak the size of a twelve-inch LP. The best way to cope with this affliction is to be prepared. Before you enter the restaurant, in fact even earlier that day, decide what you would like to have. The more specific, the better. You have been around long enough to have a pretty good idea what's on the menu. In fact, you really do not even need to look at the menu. When the waitress comes, simply tell her what you want. It's less exciting, but you won't kick yourself later.

Be Moderately Moderate

"Well," you say, "thanks for nothing! You have just taken most of the pleasure out of eating just about anything!" Maybe I have taken out some of the fun, but my motto when it comes to nutrition has always been everything in moderation—including moderation. You really do not have to give up anything entirely, even the "bad" stuff. Just eat less of it. A steak dinner, a Mexican or Chinese meal, or any other meal is not going to do you in. It's not what you eat at any one meal that is critical, it is what you eat most of the rest of the time that counts. With all of the stress in your life as it is, you don't need to add "food stress" to the list. Just be knowledgeable, be moderate, and most of all, don't be caught off guard.

KEEPING FIT

> The only reason I would take up jogging is so that I could hear heavy breathing again.
>
> —ERMA BOMBECK

Staying fit in the city can take some effort. You are constantly shifting from one task to another, and when you aren't, you want to do very little of anything else. Your opportunities for physical exercise are more limited and your resources are less accessible in the city than elsewhere. Finding a game of tennis, going for a jog, or taking a leisurely bike ride may not require careful planning in the suburbs, but in the city it becomes a big deal. And therein lies the dilemma: You have to work harder to do something you are not crazy about doing in the first place. The chances of you becoming or remaining physically fit are less than promising.

While being physically fit in the city can be a challenge, with a little time, effort, and direction you can make it happen. Here are some suggestions and ideas to speed you on your road to urban fitness.

Make the City Your Health Club

The trick is to find naturally existing outlets for activity that are readily available and easily integrated into your lifestyle and workstyle. For example, I pay a health club big bucks to let me use a machine that simulates stair climbing. For a long period I would finish my stair workouts feeling highly satisfied, yet when I'd return home after my finishing them, I would resent climbing the four flights to our apartment.

After several years it dawned on me that climbing my own stairs was not that different from climbing the StairMaster stairs. "Wow," I realized, "a free health tool right in my own home!" The point is, of course, that exercise disguised in the form of daily physical activity is all around us. The hard part is recognizing it when you see it.

Walk More

Walking is a relatively easy way of getting some exercise. As an exercise, walking has always had a wimpy reputation. But if it is done consistently, and for a sustained period of time, it can be a terrific way of staying in shape. The nice thing about walking is that it can be pleasantly camouflaged as strolling or sight-seeing—all painless. And if you crank up the pace and distance a bit, you have a wonderfully simple form of aerobic exercise that can enhance your well-being, mentally and physically. It is a great way to clear your head and calm your mind. The nice thing about walking is that you can do it pretty much anywhere, anytime, without special outfits or equipment.

But walking is more than a way of getting from place to place or even a way to exercise. In many cities, walking is one of the best ways of relating to the city. When you are not fighting gridlock, running for a bus, or trying to hail a cab, you can take a moment, look, and notice everything around you. You choose the distractions.

Climb More

There is good news, and there is better news. The good news is, research done at Johns Hopkins found that by climbing stairs for a mere six minutes a day you can add up to two years to your life. The better news is, if you live in a big city there are lots and lots of stairs. One of the things that makes big cities different from other places is the height of the buildings. While some cities are more vertical than others, all have more than their share of opportunities to climb stairs.

Most of us, given a choice between a flight of stairs and an escalator or an elevator, tend to prefer the easier route. I am not suggesting that you frenetically seek out exit doors to uncover hidden stairwells, but given a simple choice between stairs or no stairs, take the stairs.

Get Wheels

More and more we see people in the city riding their bicycles or strapping on Rollerblades. Every large city has places where you can bike and blade safely, and enjoyably. There are more in-line skating rinks and bike paths than ever before. It is a great way to get some exercise, see the city, and have a lot of fun at the same time. And please, wear your helmet.

Find the Hidden Gyms

In a big city you can work out in surprising places. There are more and more health clubs and gyms scattered around in hotels, office buildings, and apartment buildings than ever before. While these places may not be advertised, they're there. The equipment may not be elaborate, but you probably do not need elaborate. To find them you need to do a little detective work. Start with the newer apartment buildings and the bigger hotels in your area and go take a look. Some offer memberships to nonresidents and guests at a reasonable cost. Ask if some corporation in the building where you work or in a neighboring building has any health facilities. You would be surprised by the number of companies that have installed some workout equipment on their premises.

Join the Team

One of the better ways of staying in shape is taking part in a sport you enjoy. Every big city has just about every conceivable kind of sports team, from Little League to pickup games in the park on a Saturday or Sunday morning. You do not even have to be especially proficient at the sport to get onboard. Check with your local Y or community center for existing teams, or for some that may be forming in the future. Every city has some tennis courts that might have public tournament programs. Call up the parks department and see what does exist. It sure beats the StairMaster.

Remember That Every Little Bit Counts

We espouse the erroneous idea that if we do something for only a short period of time, it really is not worth doing. The reality is, if we do it consistently enough, the benefits add up. For example, a research study found that if you walk briskly for only ten minutes, three times a day, you get the same fitness and weight-loss benefits as you would if you walked briskly for thirty minutes once a day.

Parking your car a little farther from your office, and walking a little farther, day after day, month after month, can result in some fitness benefits and may even save you some parking money. Stand up and walk around. Many who live in the city work in small, often cramped offices, with highly sedentary jobs. The least you can do is take regular breaks from time to time and take small walks.

LEARNING HOW TO RELAX

Relaxation provides a relatively quick and certainly painless anti-dote for the stress and strain generated by the city. Here are some time-tested methods to release the tension in your body and quiet your mind.

Relax Your Body

Using the following simple technique, you can loosen and soothe your entire body by alternately tensing a group of muscles and then letting them relax.

Here is what to do. Start with your right arm. Make a tight fist and tense the muscles throughout your hand and arm. Hold that tension for about twenty seconds, and make yourself aware of what this tension feels like. Then, fairly quickly, release all the tension, letting your hand and arm go limp at your side. Notice the pleasant difference between that feeling of tension and the subsequent feeling of relaxation.

Now repeat this process using your left hand and arm, then your right foot and leg, and then the left. Then move to your head and face where you tighten your jaw and furrow your brow, again for about twenty seconds or so. Then let your jaw drop, and relax all the muscles of your face. Repeat this a second time. Then scrunch up your shoulders as if you were trying to use them to touch your ears. Hold that tension, and relax. What you find is that tensing and relaxing your body this way lets go of any residual physical stress. It does take some practice, but the results are well worth the effort.

Calm Your Mind

It takes but a few seconds to summon up a pleasant image or memory that can help you calm your mind. The trick is to have one ready. Take a moment to conjure up an image that you find particularly pleasing. A picture may not be enough, so try to imagine what your other senses might be picking up. What do you hear? What do you smell? What does your body feel?

The most popular images that people tend to come up with are the following:

- Imagine yourself lying on the beach in the Caribbean with a piña colada in hand, the sound of the waves lapping on the shore, the sun warming your body. You can feel the smooth sand under you. You hear the waiter announcing a buffet lunch on the beach in half an hour.
- Picture yourself relaxing by a fire, in the mountains. The snow is piled high outside. You are with someone you care very much about. You are feeling warm and cozy. You are drinking hot rum toddies.
- Mentally transport yourself into a hot bath with your favorite music in the background. Bubbles surround you. The room is candlelit. You are sipping your favorite beverage, feeling very relaxed and at peace.

If none of these do the trick, come up with your own personal relaxation image.

Try Some Beach-Ball Breathing

Proper breathing can be an incredibly effective way to reduce your body's stress. You just have to do it right. Most of us tend to breathe irregularly, too quickly, and far too shallowly. We do not allow for the proper exchange of gases in our lungs and that can leave us tense, nervous, and shaky.

The secret of stress-effective breathing is to use your diaphragm rather than the muscles in your chest. You can tell if you are putting your diaphragm to work by placing one hand on your stomach and the other on your chest. Your belly should slowly rise and fall. If the hand on your stomach barely moves, chances are you are not breathing deeply enough. Let your body breathe for you. Simply observe how your breathing slows and becomes more regular.

Here is a simple way I have found to get you to begin breathing in a more relaxing way. I call it "beach-ball breathing."

Imagine that there is a small beach ball (about the size of a grapefruit) located just behind your belly button. Also imagine that you are inflating that ball by taking in air through your belly button. (Actually, you will be taking in the air through your nostrils.) Don't overinflate, and inhale slowly and comfortably. Then slowly deflate the beach ball, letting the air escape via your belly button. (In fact, you exhale through your slightly parted lips.)

Repeat this for as long as you can. Notice the relaxed way you feel. With some practice this deeper form of breathing can become your usual way of breathing.

Get Your zzz's

The first thing you notice when you work with people under a lot of stress is just how often they say "I'm tired." For some, it is the stress of the day that wears them out. But for most others, it's a matter of simply not getting enough sleep. And they are hardly alone. The fact is, most people who live in big cities don't get enough quality sleep.

Unfortunately, when you are tired, your emotional threshold is lowered. You are more vulnerable to all the other stresses around you. Stress breeds even more stress. It becomes very important that you break the cycle and start getting a good night's sleep. Here are some suggestions.

- **Develop a Sleep Routine.** For starters, getting to bed at a sensible hour at roughly the same time each night would be helpful. Unfortunately, if you live in a big city, this is easier said than done. More happens here after the sun goes down than in other places. Still, try to hit the sheets at roughly the same time each night.

Next, it would be best if you used your bedroom for sex and sleep only. However, if you live in the city you probably do not have this luxury. You probably live in the bedroom. Instead, create a bedtime ritual. At a certain hour make the bedroom a place where you wind down and relax. This means no upsetting discussions, no work from the office, no bill paying, no arguments with the kids, no unpleasant phone calls, or anything else that might trigger worry, anxiety, and upset. You can read, watch some relaxing TV, or try some of the relaxation exercises described earlier.

- **Watch the Pills and Booze.** The quality of your sleep is as important as the amount of time you sleep. A nightcap once in a while does little harm, but heavier drinking can disturb the quality of your sleep and cause you to wake up feeling tired. Sleeping pills can be helpful when used appropriately. However, routine use of medication for sleeping can quickly become addictive and often impair sleep itself.

- **Look for Hidden Stimulants.** We tend to underestimate the effects caffeine has on our bodies. Ingesting caffeine early in the day can have lingering effects that can interfere with your sleep. The amount of caffeine in your favorite beverage can be staggering. An eight-ounce cup of drip from your neighborhood coffee bar can have up to 250 milligrams of caffeine, twice as much as your mother's cup of Maxwell House. A "grande" has up to a whopping 550 milligrams. A few of these in your system and you will stay awake until the middle of next week. Many teas, colas, and even some bottled waters have caffeine.

Some people are unaware that their medications may have stimulating side effects. A number of drugs you can buy over the counter have sleep-disrupting properties. If you are taking any form of medication and are having trouble sleeping, check with your doctor and/or pharmacist.

- **Work Out Earlier.** One would think that exercising at the end of your day would tire you and your body out, and that when your head hits the pillow, you will sleep like a baby. It doesn't work that way. Working out later in your day revs you up so that you are less likely to fall asleep. Try to get that workout in several hours before you turn out the lights.

- **Stifle Nighttime Worry.** Often when you are ready to go to sleep, you realize that you are worried, upset, angry, or otherwise distressed and this keeps you wired and awake. There are several techniques you can use to help stop this pattern of worry.

One idea is to try the "stop technique." Whenever you catch yourself obsessing or worrying incessantly about something or other, visualize a large red and white hexagonal stop sign. At the same time silently yell the word "stop" to yourself. What you find is that this temporarily interrupts your worrying. Then replace the worry with a welcome and pleasant thought or image. Keep repeating this process until you have sufficiently broken the worry cycle or have fallen asleep.

I find it useful to have a small pad and pencil near my bed. I write down the worrisome problem or thought on a piece of paper and tell myself that I will work on the problem at my office the next day. This gives me some closure and allows me to leave that little bit of business alone.

Wash Your Hands

Again, your mother was right. To stay healthy in the city it helps if you wash your hands with soap and hot water several times a day. A recent observational study of hand-washing behavior in major American cities concluded that hand washing in this country has become all but a lost art. Scientists hid in toilet stalls and counted. The city with the worst record of hand washing in a restroom was New York City (a mere 60 percent washed in Penn Station). Chicago did better: 78 percent. New Orleans had a 71 percent wash rate, San Francisco rated 69 percent, and Atlanta a poor 64 percent (during a Braves game; maybe they were in a hurry). Overall only 49 percent of the men washed compared to 89 percent of the women. Come on guys!

Use the Walk-in Clinics

In recent years there has been a growth of storefront medical services in the city. Now, recognizing the need and potential, the bigger hospitals have joined in. These walk-in health clinics can save you weeks of waiting for an appointment with another doctor. They are usually efficient, effective, and staffed by qualified medical practitioners. If you do not have your own physician, or can't wait for an available appointment, find a clinic near you.

Find a Doctor You Can Talk To

In a large city it is very easy to feel a sense of disconnection from those around you. Having a primary-care physician you trust and can confide in becomes very important. Find someone who is highly recommended and has the appropriate board certification and hospital affiliations and privileges. But it is not enough for him or her to be competent. You want a doctor with whom you feel comfortable sharing your medical concerns, someone who actually listens and hears what you are saying. You want someone who gives you enough time to ask all the questions you may have, who returns your phone calls relatively promptly, and who will make the time for you in the event of an emergency.

If you do not currently have such a doctor, ask friends if they know of somebody terrific. Arrange a short meeting and see if you feel it's a good match. If it isn't, find someone else.

8
Staying Out of Trouble

Some guy hit my fender, and I said to him, "Be fruitful and multiply,"
but not in those words.

—WOODY ALLEN

When I first came to live in New York I thought I was pretty street-smart. Looking back now, I realize that I was a peach ready for the picking. I remember strolling in the park one pleasant Saturday morning and stumbling across a small group of people huddled around a makeshift cardboard table. Behind this table was a young man rearranging the order of three cards on the table. "Find the red queen," he challenged. And I did. "Try it again," he urged. I did again. "Would you care to wager on your next guess?" You betcha! No risk here, since I had discovered that one of the cards, the queen in fact, had a bent corner. Needless to say, I left the park some forty dollars lighter and a tad wiser.

Remember that old *Hill Street Blues* caveat: "Be careful out there"? Well, it still holds. Believe it or not, there are people out there who are ill-mannered and lack basic interpersonal skills. Indeed, many of them can be downright rude and nasty. Even worse, a few of your fellow urbanites would like to bop you on the head and take everything you've got. However, a combination of street smarts, common sense, and enlightened guidance can render those mean streets less mean—and even somewhat inviting.

DEALING WITH DIFFICULT PEOPLE

Can you please tell me how to get to the Metropolitan Museum of Art or should I just go screw myself?

—Out-of-towner requesting directions

So many people, so little space, so little time. It's not surprising that sooner or later—and probably sooner—you will run into someone who will give you a hard time. In many of our bigger cities unfriendliness has become a given, an accepted part of city life. In some places, the more cynical embrace this unfriendliness with a perverse sense of civic pride. Not too long ago, I passed a large billboard ad for a new magazine. Spoofing the city's reputation for a lack of politeness, it read: WELCOME TO NEW YORK. NOW GET OUT!

Civility, it would seem, is the third casualty of big-city living (after sleep and sex). Rudeness runs rampant here. There are obnoxious clerks, hostile drivers, pushy shoppers, oblivious bicyclers, bad-mannered pedestrians, and a myriad of other difficult and unfriendly people. At some point in time you will be pushed, ignored, yelled at, kept waiting, interrupted, cut off, insulted, or otherwise treated impolitely. And while you cannot totally avoid difficult people, you can minimize your aggravation.

But maybe it is *you* who are the source of some of this discourteous behavior. To assess your own level of boorishness take this simple civility checkup quiz.

The Urban Civility Test

1. If I were on a subway or bus, and I saw a three-inch space on a seat between two already seated passengers, I would
(a) let it go and stand.
(b) look for another seat.
(c) squeeze my large backside into that space with as much gusto as I could muster, and without the slightest hint of apology.

2. If I am in my car at a traffic light, and the light turns green, and the guy in front of me doesn't immediately push the accelerator to the floor, I would
(a) patiently wait until the individual drives on.
(b) after an appropriate time, gently pat my horn.
(c) quickly hit my horn as hard as I can, show the finger, and issue an obscenity.

3. If I saw an old woman standing on the subway, and I was comfortably seated, I would
(a) immediately stand and give her my seat.
(b) ask her if she would like to sit down.
(c) carefully avoid her glances, and pretend I was a blind person.

4. Seeing that the bus was totally full, and incapable of holding even one more single passenger, I would
(a) wait until the next bus came.
(b) try another form of transportation.

(c) push and shove, making sure I got on, and also making sure that absolutely every person on that bus hated my guts and secretly wished me dead.

5. If someone, clearly from out of town, asked me for directions, I would
- (a) personally escort her to the place she was seeking.
- (b) politely give her the appropriate directions.
- (c) pretend I did not understand English, shrug my shoulders, and walk away.

6. If I were sitting on a park bench next to a frail, sickly-looking woman, and I lit up a cigarette and the woman asked me politely if would mind moving to another bench a few yards away, I would reply
- (a) "Certainly, madam, I am sorry to have disturbed you."
- (b) "No problem, and would you care for a beverage from the vendor up the road?"
- (c) "Go to hell, you old bag! If you don't like it, *you* move! Where do you people get off telling everyone what to do!"

Scoring:

Your score is simply the *total number of (c) responses.* Here is what your score means.

YOUR SCORE	YOUR RUDENESS LEVEL
0	Mama's boy!
1–3	Shows definite urban potential.
4–6	Bravo! You'll fit right in, you SOB.

You may or may not be part of the problem, but you do want to be one of those with a solution. Here is what you can do.

Expect It

Most often, you overreact whenever you are caught off guard. Let's say it has been a pretty good day, you are happily breezing along, when *whammo*, it hits you in the face. Somebody does something that pushes your button. Say, for example, someone cuts you off in traffic or sneaks in line ahead of you. Thrown off balance, you react from your gut—you feel hurt, angry, or upset. As a result, your response is usually off the mark. You either do nothing and feel aggravated, or use overkill and go for the throat.

Let's look at this another way. Suppose, magically, some soothsayer had warned you that, within the next hour, someone will push your button. Chances are, when your button was pushed, you would feel differently and react differently, able to maintain your cool while not allowing anyone to walk all over you. This time you expected something to happen. You were mentally prepared.

Hopefully, your next hour will be problem-free. However, you *will* run into some form of discourteous behavior at some point in the near future. You can bet on it. By anticipating this future experience or encounter you unconsciously replace an unrealistic expectation "Hostile, unfriendly, and rude behavior shouldn't and mustn't happen!" with the more realistic "This kind of behavior does happen, will happen, and in fact, happens all the time!" Now when something untoward does happen, you won't be caught off guard. You will be less defensive and more in control. Now you can evaluate your options and decide more sensibly the best way to respond.

Look Out for "Exclamation-Mark" Behavior

You know your expectation is unrealistic when it is accompanied by "exclamation-mark behavior." Examples of such behavior include saying any of the following to yourself when faced with the rudeness of a fellow urbanite:

"How can this be!"
"I don't understand this!"
"How could you do this!"
"I don't believe this!"
"Why would someone do this!"

What characterizes this behavior is the tone of *surprise* and *disbelief* in your reaction. Accompanying such exclamations of disbelief can be several telltale gestures. Commonly seen examples would include:

excessive eye-rolling and eyebrow-lifting
excessive and loud sighing
head shaking with accompanying *tsks*
hands thrown into the air indicating total frustration

The importance of noting this behavior is that it indicates the presence of unrealistic expectations. Implicit in your disbelief is the illogical demand: "Other people should and must be more like me. I wouldn't act like that, therefore, neither should they." But they do.

Try Some "Urban Fantasy"

A great way of making your expectations of other urbanites more realistic is to use humor and exaggeration as a de-stressing tool. It is something I call "urban fantasy." Here is how to make it work for you.

Let's say, for example, you are riding in a taxi with a driver who is clearly lost and you notice that you have just passed the same department store for the third time. You feel your level of annoyance rising to the point where you would like to hit him and cause him great pain. Using urban fantasy, you take a deep breath and imagine the following interchange:

YOU: Driver, you are totally lost. Would you please turn the meter off right now!

THE DRIVER: Absolutely! Not only that, but I will not charge you a penny for your journey. I will also pull over and ask directions, something I have never done in my entire life. I hope you have not been too inconvenienced by my inflated male ego and pigheaded behavior. I can assure you this will never, ever, happen again.

Or consider this scenario. You are on an already overcrowded elevator when it stops at the next floor. Many more people are now pushing to get on. At this point your nose is painfully embedded in the back of the person in front of you. You swing into action.

YOU: Can't you see this elevator is completely full? There's no more room! Would you *please* wait for the next one!

A SPOKESPERSON FOR THE PUSHERS AND SHOVERS: People, we were in the wrong here. Initially some of us may have thought that adding another dozen or so bodies to the group would have a minor impact. We were totally mistaken. At this point I think the best thing we can do is offer our apologies and take the stairs. You, you, and you—follow me.

The value of urban fantasy is that it can help you establish more realistic expectations of what goes on out there. Your version of what *should* happen in an ideal world is soberly replaced by what *does* happen in this less-than-ideal world. This altered perspective should result in less anger, less upset, less stress. And hopefully, the imagined interchange will bring a smile to your lips and defuse some of the anger and/or upset that was slowly building.

Cut Out the "Mind-Reading" and "Conclusion-Jumping"

We mind-read and conclusion-jump whenever we mistakenly believe we know what someone else is thinking or wrongly conclude that something is so, when in fact it is not.

Anne is a good example of a mindreader and conclusion jumper. Last Friday morning she was at the restaurant searching for some change to pay for her coffee when some guy rudely pushed ahead of her. She felt angry and saddened by how the city had become so uncaring. She didn't stop there, however. She did an instant personality evaluation, concluding that Mr. Me First was definitely a nasty piece of work, obviously a person who didn't give a damn about anybody else. Then the revenge fantasies kicked in. He was a dead man.

Moments later, mindful of his rudeness, the guy approached Anne and apologized. Not such a bad sort after all.

Anne was mind-reading and conclusion-jumping. She based her

initial reaction on a very limited bit of information. And she was wrong. In the process, she caused herself, for a short time anyway, more stress and aggravation than was necessary.

One good way of checking to see if you are mind-reading or conclusion-jumping is to do a "Perry Mason." Simply ask yourself, "Do I really have enough evidence to support my beliefs? Would a jury of my peers come back with a conviction?" If the answer is no, reconsider your case and hold off coming to any premature conclusions and reactions just yet. Who knows, you may be right, but if you are like most other people, much of the time you could be wrong.

Stop Personalizing

Carol is a personalizer. She often assumes, mistakenly, that it is *her* personality or behavior that triggers negative reactions in others. Typically, she goes home stressed out about something or other that had happened during the day. One day she went home upset that a fellow motorist had made some nasty comment about her driving. Another day she was distressed by the rude rebuke of a salesclerk who chided her for being too slow. In fact, none of this was her fault. She drives and shops better than most. Her problem was believing that she was the problem.

If you live in a big city you quickly learn that everybody has an opinion, and usually a strong one, about everything. And, more often than not, these are negative opinions that they will happily share with you. When you personalize, you fail to distinguish between opinion and fact. You assume that because people say something, or voice a criticism, they are right. Sometimes they are, but often they are not. Remember, people out there have problems. Many have disordered personalities and other forms of emotional dysfunction. Most are probably under too much stress, and certainly all have priorities that are different from yours. So before you become too distressed, stop and ask yourself, "Am I really the one at fault here?"

Watch Out for "Metropolitan Machismo"

Metropolitan machismo is a common menace in big cities. Like the bulls of Pamplona, the streets are filled with people who are brimming with hormonal excesses. I still remember the black eye on one of my patients when he came for his therapy session. Explaining his discoloration, he recounted how hours earlier, as he was crossing the street, a taxi stopped for the red light but came closer to him than he was comfortable with. My client promptly whacked the side of the cab with his fist, making a loud noise. At that point the cabbie got out of his car and punched my client. Yet another unfortunate case of "metropolitan machismo."

Recognizing people with metropolitan machismo is fairly easy. Here are some defining characteristics and typical behaviors:

1 They are mostly men (but not exclusively).
2 They become angry and hostile at the drop of a hat.
3 They see insults at every turn.
4 They are paranoid.
5 They hate backing down or losing face.
6 They get into a lot of arguments and fights.
7 They get beat up a lot.

8 They rarely eat quiche.

9 They have never heard of Alan Alda.

10 They have never read or seen *The Bridges of Madison County.*

They are out there, just hoping for some confrontation. Push them, bump them, jostle them, cut them off, insult them, or challenge them, and you are looking for trouble.

Master Urban Judo

In many ways the city can be perceived as your opponent, at times a formidable one. Given all the urban triggers out there, one could do psychological (and at times physical) battle daily. And many people do. I have always felt that too many people in the city fight too hard, too much of the time. Who needs it?

When I was in my first year at college I took a couple of semesters of judo to fulfill some phys-ed requirement. After many months of being thrown to the ground I lost my enthusiasm and abandoned any fantasies of making this a career choice.

What impressed me was not so much the physical aspects of judo but rather the underlying principles. I especially liked the notion of sidestepping rather than confronting, of using the other person's weight and energy to work for you. Later in life it also struck me that this principle and model of confrontation was a good one for psychological survival in a big city.

Mastering the elements of "urban judo" means learning how to sidestep confrontation in the city. It means, whenever possible, let it go, minimize, make up excuses, tell white lies, cross the street, look away, say "excuse me," say "I'm sorry," and get the heck away. Neutralize and minimize the interaction.

Some examples will help you better understand the concept.

THE INCIDENT	METROPOLITAN MACHISMO	URBAN JUDO
Someone pushes you on a crowded street.	Give that person a good shove back.	Walk away.
You are "dissed" on the street.	Insult right back, only do it better.	Let it go.
Another driver cuts you off.	Cut *him* off.	Drive on.
You're staring in someone's direction, and that person asks, "Who you looking at, dummy?"	"Your funny face, dumbbell!"	"Nobody."

Many of you may be thinking, "Wimp, wuss, chicken, loser." Not in my book. You are now acting city-savvy. If you think for a moment that in any of these encounters, or in ones like them, you will convince anybody of anything, change their behavior, or make your point by retaliating, you are badly mistaken. It is hard enough to change someone even when they want to change. When they don't want to, forget it. And believe me, most of your fellow urbanites do not want a lesson in civility. What you will do, however, is get yourself more angry and aggravated, and probably you'll find yourself doing something you'll regret later.

Remember this rule if you live in a big city: *Discretion* is very often the better part of assertion. Choose your battles wisely and, more often than you would like, choose to lose the battle for your own sake. In the long run, you will come out the winner.

Respond with Escalating Assertion

While avoiding and sidestepping should play a part in your urban adjustment, some situations will require a measure of assertiveness on your part. Living in a big city, I have always found that "escalating assertion" works best. This means starting out very nice, and then working your way up to ugly.

For example, you are quietly enjoying reading your newspaper in your living room when one of your neighbors turns up his or her stereo. It is loud. Very loud. You are angry, even hostile. Remembering the Stress Balance Test from Chapter Three, you quickly conclude that your response is a seven, and the situation merits a two at most. With great psychological insight you conclude that the distortion is a result of some "Can't Stand-It-itis," and a dose of unrealistic shoulds and musts on your part. You calm down, but still remain annoyed—appropriately so. Something must still be done. You decide on a strategy of escalating assertion. Here is how it works:

THE 7 STAGES	TYPICAL RESPONSES
1. "Mr. or Ms. Nice Guy."	A courteous note under their door
2. "I'm a little miffed."	A heart-to-heart phone call
3. "I'm pissed."	Personal visit; strong eye contact
4. "No More Mr. or Ms. Nice Guy."	Broom banging; threats
5. "The gloves are off!"	Police; the super; lawyer's letter
6. "Nuclear war."	Lawsuits; revenge scenarios
7. "Defeat."	Call in the movers

Start modestly and move up the action ladder. The key to escalating assertion is packaging. And the key to packaging is remaining in emotional control. Whenever you are overly upset or angry, you become a lousy packager.

Know How to Complain

Complaining in the city is a true art form, and knowing how to complain is a skill to be valued. Here are some guidelines to help you become a better complainer.

- Do complain! Most people mistakenly believe that it won't make a bit of difference. But it can. And you may be reinforcing similar complaints made by others.
- Try to first resolve the complaint with the person you have the gripe with. Then go elsewhere.
- Don't be abusive or offensive when you complain. Be firm but tactful. Though you may be dying on the inside, keep most of it in. You want to appear reasonable, credible, and determined. Turn the one you are complaining to into an ally.
- For best results go to the top, or at least higher up the ladder. They have the real power.
- If your first attempt doesn't succeed, try contacting another person. Don't give up too easily.

But don't make it your life's work either. Good luck!

STAYING SAFE AND SOUND

Never buy a Rolex watch from someone who is out of breath.
—H. JACKSON BROWN, JR.

Statistics tell us that our cities are becoming safer. Crime is down. Murders, rapes, burglaries, and robberies are all on the decline. But less crime does not mean there is nothing to worry about. The city can be a minefield where a misstep can result in a lot of grief. Becoming crime smart and street savvy is largely a matter of knowing what to look for and then knowing how to avoid it. It is partly instinctual but mostly learned.

Develop Urban Radar

The absolutely best way to avoid trouble in a large city is to see it coming. Clairvoyance would be an asset, but lacking this faculty, you need to develop a third eye and third ear. Eternal vigilance is the price we pay for living in big cities. At first this vigilance requires conscious effort, but after a while it becomes automatic.

First, learn to scan. Never become so engrossed in an activity in a public place that you are oblivious to what is going on around you. If you see people just hanging around suspiciously, or something does not seem to be the way it should, take note. Be on guard for anything that looks out of the ordinary.

Trust your instincts. Sometimes you've just got to go with your gut feelings. We can often pick up things subconsciously that our brain hasn't quite processed yet. These feelings are signaling us to pay attention. Trusting your instincts becomes especially important when you find yourself in poorly lit areas, on deserted streets, or in dangerous neighborhoods. If something doesn't feel right, there is a good chance it isn't. Never go against your intuition in the big city— it's your instinct for self-preservation telling you: Watch out!

Be Evasive

Once you suspect trouble, even a hint of it, get out of there. Cross to the other side of the street. Walk in the opposite direction. There may be nothing nasty afoot, but better safe than sorry. If you find yourself in a part of the city that is eerily deserted or looks unsafe, stay on the main roads, walk as if you know where you are going, and keep your eyes open. If someone asks you for a date or a snort, or offers you a Rolex for twenty bucks, keep right on walking. If you think you're being followed, hail a cab or go into a store or restaurant. And never be afraid to yell for help.

Make (or Break) Eye Contact

Knowing when to look someone in the eye and when not to is no simple matter. The implications of eye contact in a big city are both intricate and fascinating. There are times when making eye contact is highly appropriate. Talking to your friends, flirting, or complaining to a store clerk—all demand direct eye contact. At other times making eye contact can get you into a heap of trouble. With strangers it is generally wise to avoid locking glances. And if you don't, don't be surprised if you get a De Niro-style *"You lookin' at me?!"* in return.

Take a Pass on Pushy Panhandlers

I remember visiting Calcutta many years back and *tsk*ing at the number of beggars that accosted me in the streets. Were I to return to that city, I would hold my tongue. These days every major city has its share of indigent, homeless people on the streets asking you for money. Sadly, most of the people asking for handouts badly need the cash. Often I give something, but sometimes not. Rarely is there a confrontation. But should the person hassle you, walk away at a good clip and don't allow the situation to escalate. Remember, you are not obligated to give. In some cities there are laws governing panhandling in certain parts of the city. And if you would like to help, there are other ways of making sure your money gets into the right hands and does the most good.

Don't be intimidated. On the other hand, there's no harm in letting yourself be charmed instead. Sometimes the requests you receive on the street are very clever and elicit a smile. Raymond Alvin, a veteran observer of the urban scene, has collected a number of amusing lines designed to exact spare change from passersby. Here are three of my favorites.

- "Any spare change? My building is going co-op."
- "I'm on the road to hell. Would you help me pay the toll?"
- "I'm trying to buy Trump Tower, and I'm still a half-million short."

Don't Advertise

Crime is not totally random. A thief will look for the right opportunity before making his move. You do not have to make it easy for him. Some suggestions:

- **Your Laptop.** More than 200,000 laptops were stolen last year in this country. Avoid those black rubberized cases specially made for laptops. It's like wearing a sign on your chest that reads: I AM CARRYING AN EXPENSIVE COMPUTING DEVICE. PLEASE FIND A WAY TO TAKE IT AWAY FROM ME. THANK YOU. Insure your laptop. It's worth the premium.

- **Your Jewelry.** Save the good stuff for the inaugural ball. Or hide it under your clothing when you are in crowded public places. If you have a flashy ring, turn it around on your finger. Even an imitation Rolex can make you more popular than you want to be.

- **Your Camera.** If you have an expensive camera and use it often in places you think are risky, camouflage it by carrying it in something less eye-catching than a camera case.

- **Your Purse.** Keep it closed. If possible wear the kind that can zipper shut. Be especially careful in restaurants and other public places. Throwing your purse over your seat can make it an easy target. If you are sitting at the bar, hold it on your lap, and don't leave it on the floor where it can be easily stolen.

- **The Things in Your Car.** Keep them out of sight. Nothing is more attractive to a thief than a laptop or camera lying on the seat. Lock all doors before you leave. Better yet, take your stuff with you.

- **Your Car.** If they want your car, or your radio, or your airbags, they will get it. But you can at least make it hard for them. Get a car alarm, lock the steering wheel, get an ignition cutoff switch, and if you can't afford parking in a lot, park on a busy, well-lit block.

Don't Pull a Rambo

Unfortunately, there are no hard-and-fast rules for what to do when you find yourself in a threatening situation. The best advice is: Be very cautious. When threatened with force, always give the guy what he wants. No watch or wallet is worth your life. No brilliant repartée, no karate, no Bronsons, no Stallones.

However, there may be times when it *is* appropriate to resist, especially if you feel that if you do not resist you will be in greater physical danger. Rant, scream, yell, and kick first. Report any incident to the police and as best you can, try to remember the details of your assailant's appearance. Also, check nearby trash cans or Dumpsters for your wallet or purse. Often muggers take what they want and toss the rest away immediately.

Spot a Scam

While we are distraught and upset when we hear of a robbery or burglary, we become fascinated when we learn of a scam. Oddly, we admire a brilliant scheme that is skillfully masterminded. We loved the chicanery and double-dealing in such films as *Dirty Rotten Scoundrels* and *The Sting*. Yes, these people belong in jail, but we perversely admire how clever they are, how very good they are at what they do. Of course, you would be much less fascinated should you be the victim. So don't be. Here are some popular forms of deception that are frequently played out in the city.

• **The Ketchup Scam.** You are innocently walking along and some guy points out a mustard or ketchup stain on the back of your shirt or coat, which he put there when you weren't looking. He (or she) helps you clean it up. You are distracted. A moment later you notice that your wallet is missing.

- **The Map Trick.** This scam is usually carried out by a pair of con artists. They will approach you, requesting your help with directions at the same time they are unfolding a large, distracting map. You know what happens next.

- **The Blind-Man Scam.** I witnessed this little ruse firsthand only recently. A not-so-blind "blind" man was attempting to open the bus exit door but was having much trouble. The woman behind him, trying to help, was bending over him to push the door open. The "blind" man's accomplice behind her was attempting to take her wallet from her purse. The woman, feeling something was amiss, gave a holler and the pair fled.

- **The Elevator Drop Scam.** In this variation, the two perpetrators, looking as if they do not know one another, join you in the elevator. One of them starts a polite conversation with you, then lets her purse fall to the floor, spilling its contents. You bend down to help her and later find the other guy has taken your wallet.

The lesson? Watch out for any distraction that pulls your attention away from what you are doing. Keep your wallet in your front pocket or inside your jacket. And don't assume the crook is a bum with a five-o'clock shadow. It could be a woman or a child, or some guy in a three-piece suit. You may also want to carry your keys in a separate pocket. At least you'll be able to get inside your apartment if your bag is stolen, and you won't have to worry about someone out there who now has the keys that fit your front door and your wallet with your address inside.

Caveat Emptor

Distraction scams, however, are not the only games in town. Consider the "bait and switch" gambit. Here is how it works: You go to a store prepared to purchase the bargain-priced item prominently advertised. However, you are told: "Unfortunately, we are out of that model but we have something just as good, if not better." The salesman is convincing. Sometimes he tells you that he has the advertised model, but still steers you to something else. You purchase his selection. You may not even pay more, but he makes more. For you, the advertised item would have been the better buy.

Withdraw Carefully

ATMs can be places of trouble. If the ATM looks suspiciously quiet or desolate for any reason, you may want to pass it by. There are plenty of well-lit ATMs in the city with security guards, or at least other people in the vicinity. If you start a transaction and feel trouble is in the air, push the Cancel button, grab your card, and leave. When you are conducting any transaction, make sure you enter your PIN while standing right in front of the machine. And always take your receipt with you when you leave.

Beware of Telephone Mischief

Entering your calling card PIN while making a phone call can be riskier than you might think—especially at airports, bus stations, train stations, or any crowded public area where the telephones are easily visible. Crafty thieves have been known to obtain ID numbers using binoculars and even video cameras with telephoto lenses. They can also get numbers by standing behind callers and looking over their shoulders, or by hearing the unsuspecting callers repeat the numbers audibly to themselves. Your numbers are then offered to anyone willing to pay a bargain price for a long-distance call. You suddenly discover that your phone bill now includes calls to the newly independent province of Zakistan.

Buzz Carefully

Never let anyone into your building unless you are completely sure who they are. Crooks will claim they are UPS drivers, FedEx deliverymen, city workers, or tenants who forgot their keys. Often they will ring as many buzzers as it takes to get them inside. Go down and check in person. This will usually scare them off.

Teach Your Kid the Safety Basics

Life in the city can trigger feelings of fear and uncertainty for us grown-ups. Your kids feel no less. We could use some help, and so could they.

City hazards demand city skills. A big city has both the usual concerns any parent has living anywhere, plus very specific concerns that come with city life.

Many of us, especially those of us who have lived in large cities for a long time, have picked up our street savvy slowly, almost imperceptibly. Kids can be taught much of what we intuitively know. We just have to target the learnings and package it well.

The best way of teaching kids how to handle situations is to role-play them, acting out the different options. Rehearse what to do if they are lost or if they feel they are being followed, or if someone tries to touch them. Bad things can happen anywhere, not just in the city. However, the chances of these misfortunes happening are probably greater in big cities. Therefore, precautions are essential.

Try Not to Watch the Local News

A couple of years ago a *Los Angeles Times* poll found that the way people feel about crime is based largely on what they see and read in the media. In reality, unless you are a card-carrying member of the crime world, your chances of being murdered are probably about the same as they were twenty-five years ago.

Unless you have a very specific reason for watching the local news, such as you were voted Citizen of the Year or you are sure you are this week's Lotto winner, avoid it. The local news can fuel a higher degree of anxiety and fear than is appropriate. You do not need the fire, rape, or murder du jour to add to your already stressful day. Change the channel.

Stop Worrying So Much

Any large city can be a frightening and intimidating place, especially if you believe that the city is more dangerous than it really is. There are risks to living in a big city. However, most people exaggerate those risks, and in the process cause themselves a great deal of unnecessary stress.

We get incredibly worked up over the dangers of alar on our apples, asbestos in our ceilings, and benzene in our Perrier, but neglect the real dangers of being overweight, driving a car, and not getting a regular physical exam. We underestimate the common risks but exaggerate the ones that are highly unlikely. We become frightened, but by the wrong things. The fact is, your chances of experiencing serious harm or injury is far, far smaller than your worrying would justify. Can I absolutely guarantee that you will not be a victim of foul play? No. Would I bet big money that this will not happen to you? Yes. Don't go bananas.

9

Connecting with Others

Should I marry W.? Not if she won't tell me the other initials in her name. And what about her career? How can I ask a woman of her beauty to give up Roller Derby? Decisions . . .

—WOODY ALLEN

I distinctly remember the way I felt those first days and weeks being alone in a new, very large city. I was bipolar—either miserable or ecstatic. My moods would change with disturbing frequency. One moment I would feel lonely, disconnected, and ready to leave. A moment later I would be raving about the glories of the urban experience. Clearly I was not to be trusted.

These feelings were fueled by alternating hopes and anxieties. First I'd feel hope: "With all those people out there, surely you will meet someone," then anxiety: "You will live in your suitcase-sized apartment, alone, forever." Eventually everything worked out terrifically well. I made friends, got married, had kids, made more friends, and even found a bigger apartment.

To reduce the sense of alienation one can feel living in a large city, it is important that you develop feelings of connectedness and involvement with those around you. Your relationships with others give you a sense of belonging to something larger, something stronger. Being with friends and acquaintances, those you care about and who care about you, can act as stress buffers, easing the pressures of the city and providing you with support and comfort. You want to build a network of social relationships and communal support that extends from nodding acquaintances to caring friends and intimate lovers. You want to have people you can be with, talk with, laugh with, cry with, and yes, at times even sleep with.

MEETING PEOPLE

Elaine: Jerry, if you do that they're going to ostracize you from the community!

Jerry: Community? What community? You mean I've been living in a *community* all these years!? I had no idea!

—from an episode of *Seinfeld*

Being alone in a big city can be hard. We need all the friends we can get. But how do we find these people? While the numbers would suggest that it is easy to meet people in a big city, one can live a lifetime there without really connecting. Yet with the right motivation and effort it can happen before you know it.

I have found that some of the biggest obstacles to meeting new people in the city are our old attitudes and assumptions. These time-worn internal rules act as roadblocks, slowing the process and in some cases making it almost impossible to get involved with others. Many of these beliefs are subconscious or unconscious, and we are barely aware of how they operate. But they do.

Here are some of the more important misguided myths about the ways we should meet new people. See if any of these ring a bell.

The Three Most Common People-Meeting Myths

1. *The Myth:* Meeting people should happen naturally and spontaneously.
   The Reality: Maybe it would be if you lived in Mayberry with Opie and Aunt Bee. More often than not, meeting new people in the city is a deliberate and often contrived process.

2. *The Myth:* It is much harder to make friends in a large city than it is in a small town.
   The Reality: Big cities offer far more opportunities to meet new people than towns or even smaller cities. It just seems harder.

3. *The Myth:* I should feel comfortable and at ease when I meet new people.
   The Reality: That would be nice. Most often we feel some nervousness and discomfort when we meet new people, at least at first.

Make a conscious decision to start with an open mind. Be willing to look at any new ideas and suggestions, no matter how radical, brash, or even silly they may seem at the time. You do not necessarily have to agree with all of them, just consider them, try more than a few, and see for yourself whether they work or not. Start with a clean slate.

Get a Life

The best way to find other people is to build a lifestyle that is involving, interesting, and puts you in contact with others. Daily we slide right past dozens of people, many of whom would be delighted to know us if they but had the chance. Give them that chance. Become active in your community. The more you get involved, the better your chances of meeting someone you would like to spend time with.

Join the Group

Every major city has numerous groups and organizations that can put you together with other like-minded city dwellers. By sharing a common interest you establish a natural bond that can transform your relationship with others in the group from mere acquaintances to good friends. Here are some groups you may want to consider belonging to:

- your local church or temple
- your child's school (PTA, class parent, fund raiser, safety patrol)
- your block association
- your co-op or condo association
- a special interest group (a book group, a nature group, a music group, a political group, a singles group)

Or learn something. One advantage of living in the city is the access you have to the many classes and courses offered. Some suggestions:

- city universities, colleges, and community colleges
- the Y
- the Learning Annex
- language classes
- craft schools
- cooking classes
- writing classes
- aerobics classes
- dancing lessons
- music lessons

Or consider getting involved in a game or sport. Try:

- bridge
- golf
- poker
- mah-jongg
- lawn bowling
- bowling
- billiards
- swimming
- gymnastics
- ice-skating
- softball
- basketball
- volleyball
- hockey
- bingo
- scuba diving

Step Forward

One of the best ways to meet new people and feel that you are a part of the community is to become a volunteer. You do not have to be a Mother Teresa, or invite strange families to come live with you. You can start small. You might, for example:

- volunteer to help out at a local homeless shelter
- help out at a library
- help at the museum (tour assistant, fund-raising guide)
- improve a neighborhood garden, park, or sidewalk
- coach kids in some team sport
- deliver food to the homebound or the elderly
- become a tutor in the public school system
- become a big brother or sister
- help administer a favorite charity
- help out at the ASPCA or other animal organization
- help organize a blood drive
- be part of a hotline
- teach literacy for adults
- become part of an ESL (English as a second language) program
- help with fund-raising at a radio or television station
- work at a nursing home
- be a helper at a day-care center
- assist at a senior citizen center

Often the biggest obstacle to volunteering is figuring out what to do and where to go. Most larger cities have one or more umbrella organizations or clearinghouses that are aware of all the volunteering opportunities in the city. To find it, call up any major volunteer group. They will know where to send you.

Market, not Mall

Last summer Beth and I were lucky enough to be invited to spend a week in Provence with some friends who had rented a charming one-hundred-year-old farmhouse. Each morning we would walk to the neighboring town where we would sit in a small cafe and have strong coffee and fresh croissants. We would then go marketing, stopping for bread and desserts at the bakery, meat at the butcher shop, vegetables at the greengrocer, flowers at the flower market, and wine at the winery. I cannot think of a more inefficient way of managing my time. It was wonderful.

One of the pleasures of living in a big city is being able to do your chores and errands in a way that combines the charm of a village or small town with the choice and diversity that only a larger city can offer. When you live in the city, the *process* of day-to-day self-maintenance is valued as much as the result.

Shopping at smaller stores and using local services may take more time and effort, but the payoff can be gratifying. Patronize your local merchants and shopkeepers. Get to know their stores and their services. And get to know the people who work there. You want their faces to become familiar, faces you come to recognize and that greet you with a smile of recognition. Over time these relationships build a feeling of connectedness and a greater sense of community. These became *your* stores.

FINDING URBAN ROMANCE

Famous writer needs woman to organize his life and spend his money. Loves to turn off Sunday football and go to botanical gardens with that special woman. Will obtain plastic surgery if necessary.

—JOE BOB BRIGGS, *Sure-fire Singles Ads*

It has been said that everyone who lives in a big city is looking for at least one of three things: a new place to live, a new job, or a new relationship. Most often it is finding the latter that evokes the most grief. The thought of having to actively meet someone for purposes of romance can make grown men and women cringe. Other than undergoing colonoscopy or preparing for a tax audit, there is probably no other time in our lives when we experience as much reluctance and distress. We want the end result, the romance, but hate the process needed to get there.

I wish I could say that finding the person of your dreams is always easy. I'm sure that more than one or two people have found that special him or her quite effortlessly. It could have been a guy in their step class or a woman they met at a friend's party. Most of the rest of us find meeting others far more arduous and less magical, and frankly, quite a pain.

Everything we said about meeting people and making new friends applies to meeting a mate for life. The difference is, you have to be even more determined, more committed, and most important, more gutsy.

Forget Jane Austen

In all those Jane Austen novels, meeting eligible people seemed so easy. The process was so wonderfully structured and formalized. No need to waste your time pub-hopping or placing a singles ad in the local *Shropshire Gazette*. All a woman had to do was wait in the parlor while prospective mates would be ushered in for her inspection. True, she had to needlepoint until her fingers ached something fierce, and sometimes she could wait years for the right squire to show up, but most everyone seemed happily paired by the end of Austen's books.

Will that approach work for you in the big city? I don't think so.

Stop "Yes, but-ing"

When I first started practicing as a therapist I fell into more than my share of new-therapist traps. Working with singles, the one that most often snared me was the "Yes, but" trap. It works something like this. First I'd come up with what I thought was a reasonable idea where and how my patient might meet someone. The patient would listen but would immediately respond with "Yes, but . . ." and proceed to tell me why that idea would not work. Then I would come up with another idea. The patient would again come back with another "Yes, but . . ." This mutually frustrating interchange continued until one of us tired, usually me.

The Ten Most Commonly Heard Excuses for <u>Not</u> Going Out to Meet Someone

1 "I tried that already. A waste of time."

2 "All the good ones are married or gay."

3 "It's a meat market out there."

4 "Men are only after one thing."

5 "Women are looking for guys with a lot of bucks."

6 "Everybody is too young."

7 "Everybody is too old."

8 "They're all losers at places like that."

9 "If it's meant to happen, it'll happen on its own."

10 "What's the use? I'll never meet the right person."

There are dozens and dozens of reasonable-sounding excuses not to meet people with relationship potential. Most contain at least a sliver of truth. All will immobilize you.

Explore Anyplace, Anywhere, Anytime

Forget the notion that there is a right time and place to meet that special someone. There isn't. Consider these *un*romantic venues as potential opportunities:

- on the bus
- at the health club

- in the supermarket checkout line
- waiting for the subway
- having a cup of coffee
- buying a newspaper
- in your dentist's waiting room
- in your therapist's office (. . . maybe not)
- in the bookstore
- in a card store
- in a museum
- at a flower stand
- at a nice hotel
- in church, temple
- at a drugstore
- at a gallery opening
- at a video store
- at a post office
- at a fund-raiser
- at a library (but quietly)
- at an ATM (but cautiously)

Once you have spotted someone you might want to meet, bite the bullet and take a risk.

Make Your Move

The major roadblock to meeting someone is our fear of rejection. Nobody likes rejection, but if we entirely avoid situations where we might experience it, we greatly limit our chances of meeting someone. Ask yourself: "What's the worst that can happen? He or she will say no?" You can learn to live with that.

Remember that when you're still alone on your deathbed at the age of ninety-seven, you will not regret the risks you took or any rejection you encountered because of it. You will regret, however, not having taken more of them. Look for opportunities to take risks, and take them.

Flirt

Hands down, flirting is the most efficient and effective way of meeting someone. By flirting I mean:

1. *Make eye contact*—Don't stare. Simply lock eyes for a brief second or two.
2. *Smile*—Slightly, not ear to ear. Then say something.

This goes, of course, for both men and women.

Break the Ice

All of us have admired that social smoothie who, in just about any situation, is able to come up with a bon mot or that morsel of wit that immediately catapults him or her into the inner circle, while we cower on the periphery thinking, "I wish I had said that."

Fortunately, you do not have to come up with that brilliant one-liner that will reduce him or her to paroxysms of laughter. Don't overthink. You do not have to be dazzling. The stress of trying to come up with that zinger will usually leave you frozen and mute. Think of what you will say as simply a way of getting your foot in the door. Ask a question. Give a compliment.

Once the conversation has started you can take it anywhere else you wish. Just start talking. Do try to make your overtures open-ended and where possible, avoid questions with a yes or no answer. Then, assuming there is sufficient interest, give him or her your business card and say how nice it would be if you got together for coffee or something.

Work with a Prop

Sometimes having an accessory can work as a social lubricant, facilitating the meeting process. Here are some field-tested suggestions.

The Six Most Effective Props to Help You Find Romance in the City

1 An adorable child[1]
2 A cute pet[2]
3 One or two current bestsellers[3]
4 An easel, canvas and paint, or a sketch pad[4]
5 A camera[5]
6 A laptop computer[6]

[1]A smallish child, borrowed for the day, can work nicely. The cuter the better. Make it very clear early on that you are the child's uncle or aunt and *not* the parent.

[2]Puppies work best. Unless you are going for a menacing De Niro look, avoid snakes and reptiles entirely. Birds will get people to talk to you, but you will be dangerously close to looking "marginal."

[3]In those early moments do not actually read the book. Look like you just put it down and are "open for questions and discussion."

[4]Some talent is a definite plus.

[5]An even better idea is to get ahold of a 35mm movie camera and one or two assistants and give the impression that you are making a movie . . . nah, too complicated.

Advertise

Personal ads can be an effective weapon in the war against single-dom. A patient of mine placed an ad in a city magazine and received ninety-nine replies. After some eleven dinners, five lunches, twenty-one coffees, and nine drinks dates, he is now happily involved with one of the responders.

The latest twist on the personal ad is the coffee bar fix-up. Think of it as Starbucks with a social director, a Central Perk where the bartender plays cupid. You fill out a form listing all your vitals and preferences. Dozens of others do the same. This is converted into a personal ad, which is posted in a large book or on a bulletin board. You peruse and select a description that captures your fantasy. No names are listed, just ID numbers. The bartender calls up your choice and sees if there is any mutual interest. If there is, a meeting is set up at the coffee bar, and you get to know each other better sipping a skim, no-foam, decaf, mocha frappuccino.

Try a Dating Service

Using a dating service can be an effective and efficient way of meeting people. Personal interviews, computerized matching, and video introductions can all reduce the chances of meeting people that you would immediately reject. There are even personalized dating services that, like a career headhunter, will work for you on an individual basis, placing ads and doing the legwork.

But before you plunk down your hard-earned cash, ask a prospective service for their brochure and a description of their clients—ages, occupations, geography, etc. Ask about the number of "dates" you are entitled to, how often you will meet someone, and how much money you will get back if you are unhappy with the service. Check with the Better Business Bureau for a list of previous complaints about their organization.

DE-STRESSING CITY SEX

> It's been so long since I made love I can't even remember who gets tied up.
>
> —JOAN RIVERS

Sex. We think about it, read about it, joke about it, and worry about it. We see it everywhere, selling us undershorts and soda pop, magazines and movie tickets. If you live in a big city, the place where you may not see much of it is in your own bedroom. The cliché "Not tonight dear, I have a headache" is currently undergoing a revival. But this time there is a difference. The headache now is genuine and it could be the guy who is bowing out. The cause? You guessed it: city stress.

Headaches are but one of the many stress-related reasons that city dwellers use to explain their lowered libidinal interest. Here is a short list of some of the more common excuses I hear when I talk to urban couples about their sex lives:

- "I'm too anxious."
- "I'm too upset."
- "I'm too angry."
- "I'm too depressed."
- "I'm too worried."
- "I'm too busy."
- "Let's watch the news first."
- "The kids will hear us."
- "I'm too tired."
- "I have no energy."
- "I need my sleep!"
- "I'll just rest my eyes first."
- "I'll get AIDS!"
- "I'll get herpes!"
- "I'll get something!"
- "I've got something!"

You probably can list one or more of the above statements that for you has resulted in another night of missed intimacy. More and more city folk feel that their stressful lives in the city are preventing them from enjoying one of life's most basic and natural pleasures. More important, their relationships are at risk. When sex becomes a casualty, intimacy, trust, and caring are also threatened. Distressed sex becomes the red flag that signals more serious problems to come. So, before you get to that point . . .

Learn to Unwind

Unwinding and reducing any residual tension and worry becomes an important step in regaining sexual interest. Finding ways of segueing into a more sexual state of mind would surely help. For many of us, getting into that sexy mood takes a bit of doing. Shifting gears is not easy. It's been a long day. There are a million and one things going on in your lives. Worries and concerns are filling your head. Having sex may not be your top priority. This means you have to learn how to relax your body and turn off your mind. Anxiety, anger, worry, upset—all are natural antagonists that distract you from sex. Your mind detours and takes your body with it.

There are a number of ways to help you unwind and release some of that stress. One of the best is a mutual massage, which can quickly take a turn for the sexy. Try a massage with some silky aromatic oils. It is a wonderful way of moving from the routine to the romantic, dissipating any tension in the process. A hot shower or bath, solo or with your partner, can be wonderfully soothing. Simply sitting in your favorite chair listening to calming music can often do the trick.

One way of getting "into the mood" is to start by yourself. Begin fantasizing about making love and finding yourself in the throes of passion. It's surprising how once you start down this road, you find that your sexual interest grows very quickly. A suggestive video can also turn your thoughts away from the politics at the office. Experiment.

Make the Time

Sex takes time. True, for many of us in the city, time is what we are short of most these days. But you still have to find it. Of course, we can't do it all. Many of us suffer from the misguided expectation that we can work a full day, prepare meals, take care of the kids, read the paper, watch Leno, Letterman, or the late news, have terrific sex, and go to sleep. It almost never works.

And you can guess what gets left out most of the time. Our intentions are good, but our follow-through is faulty. We really believe there is enough time for everything, especially sex. We find ourselves repeating the same pattern of nightly behavior, with the same consequences. And no matter how often it happens, it's always a bit of a surprise to us. We think, "It's too late to do anything else. I guess it's time to go to bed. Maybe tomorrow." But tomorrow is a rerun of today. And that's what makes this effect so interesting. We really believe every night will be different, and it rarely is.

If there is any sex in the city, it usually happens on weekends. But not always. Too often the week spills over into the weekend, and those well-intended plans for sex slip by. As one of my patients put it, "The weekend is when we do our socializing. We like to go out on Friday and Saturday nights, even if it's just dinner and a movie. The problem is, we come home late, plop into bed, turn on the TV, and go to sleep. When we do have sex, it is often hurried and over pretty quickly. It's okay, but not great. I guess we just need a longer day!"

Make a Date

Spontaneity is wonderful, but frankly it is overrated. We misguidedly expect sex to happen at unplanned, magical moments. And it will. Unfortunately, your next moment may be March 5, 2005. You may not want to wait that long.

My advice? Supplement your spontaneous lovemaking. Pre-plan your sexual encounters. Make a date to be intimate with your partner. You ask, "How can the experience be terrific if it is set up like a business meeting?" Think of it as making a reservation at your favorite restaurant. You enjoy the meal no less because it is an entry in your organizer. In fact, you anticipate and get excited about the prospect hours before.

Keep Out the City

Making love in a cabin in the woods is one thing; making love in a big city is something else again. There is nothing like the whining of a car alarm to arrest all passion and rob you of the mood.

Turn off the TV, disconnect your beeper, unplug your fax, take the phone off the hook, use your answering machine (with the volume off), and mask any street noise with soothing music. Don't assume that because it is quiet when you start, it will stay quiet.

10

Thriving in the City

The key to urban living is to rejoice in urban virtues.

—CELIA GUILD

*R*ecently I bumped into a friend who had just moved back into the city after many years of living in the suburbs. Curious, I asked her why she had come back. She smiled. "The action," she confessed. She missed the hustle and bustle of the city and the vitality of life here. I knew exactly what she meant.

While I was pleased by her eager return to the city, I also remembered how easy it is to lose that sense of enthusiasm. While a big city has the ability to enchant, charm, and amuse us, the strains of metropolitan life can slowly outweigh any positive feelings we might have felt for it. The honeymoon is soon interrupted by the realities of day-to-day existence, and urban pleasures are quickly lost in the city shuffle. We lose the ability to extract joy from the city.

Thriving in the city means deriving pleasure and happiness from those things that make a city a city. You must discover what the city has to offer and build a repertoire of experiences, involvements, and associations that can provide you with a sense of delight, joy, and satisfaction. It also means finding time for yourself, time to regain your emotional equilibrium. Solitude and privacy are rare commodities in the city, but they are essential if you want to maintain your sanity and refresh your soul.

Most important, thriving in a big city means finding the right balance. You have to learn how to balance the energy, excitement, and chaos of the city with periods of retreat, withdrawal, and, at times, escape.

ENJOYING CITY PLEASURES

If it weren't for pickpockets, I'd have no sex life at all.

—RODNEY DANGERFIELD

Whenever friends or relatives come to visit I am always reminded of just how wonderful living in a big city can be. When they visit it becomes our job to show them the town and make sure they have a good time. We take them to see things and do things that we normally never would. And not surprisingly, *we* begin to get excited about the city. Everyone, especially us, has a great time. We vow to do it again, soon, and without the guests. But we rarely do.

Even the most enthusiastic city-boosters need a shot in the arm from time to time. We lose sight of the fact that our relationship with the city is much like any other relationship. It takes work to make it thrive. It has to be nourished, nurtured, and above all, never taken for granted.

(Re)discover the City

Become a tourist in your own city, even if you have lived there for the last fifty years. See what other people see when they come to your city. Take a look or a second look at what makes your city interesting and exciting. No matter how clichéd the attraction, go take a look. There is probably a good reason why the attraction became a cliché.

Get ahold of a good map to help you get around. Even before you leave your living room, a map can give you a sense of familiarity and access to your city. Then start exploring. If you take the car make sure at some point you get out of the car and start walking. Nothing gets you closer to life in a city than walking in one. The best way to get to know a neighborhood, new or old, is to stroll its streets. Walking allows you to control the speed and rhythm of your journey. You are able to luxuriate in all the glorious detail, be it a building facade, a shop window, or simply an interesting face that passes by.

Go Buy the Book

Go to your favorite bookstore and head for the travel section. Most of the larger city bookstores carry a good selection of books about their own city. Guidebooks these days are far more inviting and fun to read than the ho-hum versions we remember from years ago. Some of the more offbeat titles that caught my eye on my last trip to the bookstore included:

- *A Vegetarian's Guide to the City*
- *The City at Night*

- *A Guide to Volunteering in the City*
- *Romantic Days and Nights in the City*
- *A Dog Owner's Guide to the City*
- *A Walker's Guide to the City*
- *A Bike-Rider's Guide to the City*
- *A Guide to Ethnic Restaurants in the City*
- *A Gay Guide to the City*
- *A Single Person's Guide to the City*

Check In

One great way of discovering the interest and excitement that your city offers is to take a minivacation right in the city. In most bigger cities, hotels have special weekend rates, far lower than the usual rate. Check your newspaper to find where the bargains are, choose an appealing hotel, and check in. Get all the tourist information that hotels have lying around and ask all those questions tourists are supposed to ask. Then start exploring, doing all the things you normally never would.

Take the Tour

Our friend Jeff celebrated his fiftieth birthday by giving some family members and friends a guided bus tour of the city. His purpose was to reminisce, revisiting those parts of the city that were important in his life. While it was fun to see where Jeff went to school, courted his wife, raised his family, and ate lunch, I must admit I was more fascinated by the other parts of the tour. Our knowledgeable guide regaled us with tidbits of local history, architectural footnotes, and juicy scraps of celebrity gossip. All in all it was a wonderful afternoon. By the end of the day my batteries felt recharged. I was excited about the city again.

Every large city has such tours. Find one and take it. Your tour may be less personal, and certainly without the cake and candles, but it will probably be as interesting.

Pick Up Some History

Usually, the more we know about something, the more we like it. When you know something about the history of a place, a building, a neighborhood, it becomes more meaningful to you and you become more connected to it.

The history need not be of the high school variety. It could be a literary history, describing which notable writers and authors lived when and where. Or a social history showing you which performers, artists, and movers and shakers lived in the city at various times. Your neighborhood will feel somehow different when you know that a favorite writer or celeb grew up but a few blocks away. You may never look at those streets and buildings in quite the same way again.

Become an Insider

Discover the city as only someone who lives in that city can. Go beyond the usual guidebook and tourist standbys. Get to know the city at another level. Find out where those marvelous off-the-beaten-track restaurants are located, and which of the smaller galleries, museums, clubs, and shops are worth repeated visits. But you may already be an urban maven. Complete this little quiz and see.

Where in your city would you go to:

Eat a truly great hamburger   _____

See a classic old movie   _____

Hear music in a piano bar   _____

See interesting photography   _____

Eat great french fries   _____

Eat the best pizza   _____

Find a great place to jog   _____

Find the best used bookstore   _____

Get the best city view   _____

Ride a bike   _____

Ride a horse   _____

Sit at a sidewalk bistro   _____

Find a great diner   _____

Find a farmer's market   _____

Hear super jazz   _____

See a good play inexpensively   _____

Go ice-skating   _____

Find a great flea market   _____

Get Off the Couch

"Use it or lose it," that old nostrum of sex therapy, applies to cities as well. The less you make use of the city, the less pleasure and satisfaction you derive from it. Unfortunately, it seems as if we have a lot of trouble leaving our homes. We like staying in our own backyard (assuming we have one). We love just staying in. Many of us think we use the city, but we are often mistaken. How about you?

When was the last time you

- went out for dinner?
- went out to a movie?
- went dancing?
- saw a play?
- heard a concert?
- people-watched?
- went to a nightclub?
- strolled in the park?
- went shopping just for fun?
- explored a new neighborhood?
- saw a dance performance?
- went to a sports event?
- had lunch out with friends?
- went to a museum?
- went to an art gallery?

Discover Simpler City Pleasures

Much of our happiness comes from the small bits of pleasure and satisfaction we experience. By themselves, each is no big deal. Yet, taken together, these simpler, smaller pleasures contribute to a larger positive feeling we may have about ourselves and our city. These are what I call "hassle insulators," the not-so-terribly-significant involvements and activities that can insulate you and protect you from the bigger stresses of city life. Here are some suggestions:

- Find an outdoor cafe in your neighborhood and just dawdle for a while.
- Banter with a store clerk.
- Spend a couple of hours at the public library.
- Sit on a park bench and people-watch.
- Explore a neighborhood that is new to you.
- Cover up and go for a walk when it is raining.
- Buy yourself some flowers.
- Buy an ice cream or frozen yogurt on the street.
- Buy a hot dog from a local street vendor.
- Read the newspaper and have a cup of coffee at a coffee bar.
- Strike up a conversation with a stranger.
- Listen to a street musician (and give him / her something).
- Go walking or jogging in the park.
- Browse in a flea market.
- Go to a street fair.
- Have a meal at an outdoor restaurant.

The possibilities are limited only by your imagination.

Experiment and Take Risks

Here are some additional ideas and suggestions to add to your repertoire of urban activities and involvements. These are a little offbeat, some may be a bit of a stretch, but all are rewarding and worth the effort.

Thirty-one Things You Should Do at Least Once in the Big City

1. Attend a religious service *not* of your own faith.
2. Fly over the city in a helicopter.
3. Shoot pool in a billiard parlor.
4. Join a softball team that plays in the park.
5. Go folk dancing outdoors.
6. Join an Easter procession at a Greek Orthodox church.
7. Rollerblade in the city.
8. Take a bicycle tour of your city.
9. Go to a dog (cat, horse) show.
10. Go English country dancing.
11. Picnic somewhere right in the city.
12. Take a professional cooking course.
13. Learn a foreign language with a group of people.
14. Go to a comedy club.
15. Go Texas line-dancing.
16. Take tea in the fanciest hotel in town.
17. Go bowling.
18. Go hear a concert in the park.
19. Go to the Fourth of July fireworks display.
20. Go for a carriage ride in the city.
21. Walk to work.
22. Ride your bike to work.
23. Second-act a play (sneak in at intermission).
24. Go to the park at night immediately after a new snowfall.
25. Stay out all night and catch the sunrise.
26. Go to a Turkish or Russian bathhouse.

27. Have breakfast in a swanky hotel dining room.

28. Go to Midnight Mass in a cathedral at Christmas.

29. Sleep out in your backyard, on your terrace, or on your roof.

30. Take a kid to the zoo.

31. Make love in a public place with no one around.

Go for it.

FINDING A QUIET RETREAT

I never said, "I want to be alone." I said, "I want to be left alone."
—GRETA GARBO

A big city can provide you with just about everything and anything you might want or need. Everything, it seems, but a little peace and quiet, and some time to yourself. Getting away from it all is not easy. True solitude, in the sense of complete isolation, is nearly impossible to come by. There are very few opportunities to be completely alone once you leave your home. However, relative solitude and a greater sense of seclusion, privacy, and quiet is possible—even if there are a few other people around.

Not everyone, of course, needs or wants to be off by themselves. In fact, over the last few hundred years, solitude has gotten a bad rap. There was a time when being alone was regarded as something positive, something to be desired. Not anymore. Wanting to be alone now has acquired a definite antisocial ring to it. Many believe it to be a little strange, at best. At worst, a sign of pathology. In this country it is regarded as downright un-American. Why would anyone want to be alone?

Yet being alone, as many of us know, can be joyous. Being in your own head, away from everyone—daydreaming, planning, imagining—can be incredibly involving and wonderfully satisfying. Rather than something to be shunned, solitude should be cherished. Living in a big city with all the turmoil and confusion makes time alone that much more precious. True, it may only be for a few minutes, but those minutes can go a long way.

Learning to appreciate solitude and time for yourself takes some practice. Start gradually. Reading by yourself is often a good way to begin. Turn off the TV, radio, and anything that might be distracting. Find a place where you can be alone and quietly read. Later, experiment with meditative exercises or being alone without a prop—no book, no nothing. It is an acquired pleasure, but well worth the effort. Greta got it right. Sometimes we just want to be left alone.

Create an Inner Sanctum

Try to create a space within your home that you really like to spend time in. Have at least one "feel good" room or area that is emotionally welcoming. Your private corner can be anyplace. It could be as simple as a window seat, or a warm kitchen, an inviting bedroom, or a cozy study where you can close the door and feel away from it all.

For many city folk, the bathroom may be the only place in their home where they can lock the door and be alone. A hot bath is a wonderful way to relax and totally let go. Stretched out and surrounded by warmth, here we can give ourselves permission to do nothing but relax. Adding some soft lighting, gentle music, and a soothing drink can make this feel like heaven.

All you need is a little space where you feel unhurried and hassle-free. This is your inner sanctum, a space within a space to which you can retreat when the world outside feels less than hospitable, a place where you can sit, read, write, think, or just daydream. Designate this space as one in which you do not worry, pay bills, answer the phone, or do anything else that could even remotely increase your level of stress. The rewards of having a quiet place to retreat are immense.

Park Awhile

I hope you live close to a park. And I hope you make use of it. But even if there isn't one close by, make an effort to get to know many of the nicer parks in your city. Every major city has many wonderful parks where you can stroll aimlessly, taking in the activity around you or becoming lost in your own thoughts and images. In the city's larger parks you can often find yourself quite alone, one of the few places in the city where there is no one else around. When I can, I find walking through the park on the way to my office or coming home after work a wonderful way of mellowing out and disassociating from the city and my busy day.

Miniparks are far more numerous. Sometimes they are no more than a small patch of grass, a few trees, and a bench or two. But on the right day and at the right time, they can be relatively empty and provide you with some peace and quiet.

Jogging, bicycling, or Rollerblading in the park are great ways of combining exercise with a sense of solitude. You can bring a Walkman or, better yet, simply enjoy being alone with your thoughts.

Seek Sanctuary

We tend to think of houses of worship as religious sanctuaries, places for prayer. They are, of course, but churches and temples can also be visited for nonreligious expression. You can reflect, meditate, or simply lose yourself in reverie. They are quiet and softly lit—ideal settings to be alone. Many are quite majestic and sweeping in their architectural grandeur, inspiring and revitalizing even to the most city-worn spirit. And except for times such as Christmas Midnight Mass and Yom Kippur, your chances of finding an empty pew are pretty good.

Look for Water

Many, if not most, of our bigger cities are located on the shores of oceans, lakes, or rivers. One of the reasons they grew to become cities was that they were accessible by water. With a bit of scouting you can almost always discover a quiet area overlooking the water. Usually the city has provided benches and even tables for its citizens. If not, it's a good idea is to keep a folding chair or picnic blanket in the trunk of your car.

Find a Sunset

My favorite part of the day is that time when the sun is just setting. The time between day and evening can be gloriously hypnotic. Finding sunsets in the city may not be an easy matter. But they do exist. Find a number of spots where you can savor the last moments of your day. The results can be tranquilizing. I would also have suggested a sunrise, but frankly I am rarely up early enough. You, however, might be an early riser. Try it.

Become a Lobbyist

Many of the city's hotels, especially some of the older ones, are wonderful buildings that can be a treat to spend time in. You won't be alone there, but chances are you will be left alone. While there can be much coming and going, don't be surprised if you find a comfortable chair situated in a relatively quiet part of the lobby.

An atrium in a large office building or museum, a plaza, or any large open space are other sources of relative solitude. Many supply tables and benches that offer passersby a place to eat lunch, read the paper, or people-watch.

Visit the Animals

Zoos and aquariums make excellent places to escape most humans. When visited on a weekday, they are relatively empty. Fish, by nature, tend to be fairly quiet. Watching them swim slowly and effortlessly can be a relaxing experience. Most animals will evoke a smile, a laugh, or a feeling of tenderness.

And don't forget your animals at home. Playing for even a few minutes with a cat or dog or ferret, or even watching your goldfish, can reduce your stress level and allow you time to regroup and regain your equilibrium.

Cultivate Solitude

As the urban gardener Linda Yang points out, the word *paradise* comes from the Persian cum Greek *paradeisos*, meaning private park of kings—where there was peace and beauty amid fruit-bearing trees and flowers. A few square yards of such a paradise can bring some tranquillity to your life.

Working in a garden can be satisfying. Your garden need not be extensive. It could be a small terrace, a shared plot of ground, an indoor herb garden in the winter months, or simply several house-plants that you water and prune. The effect is the same. Beth and I have some planters on the roof and relish the chance to putter and pot.

Lose Yourself in the Shelves

When the mega-acreage bookstores started taking over the city I became fearful. Surely, I reasoned, the demise of my small neighborhood bookstore was around the corner. As it turned out, "around the corner" proved to be the operative phrase. A mammoth Barnes & Noble opened a mere two blocks away and within a year my favorite bookstore was gone. I was devastated.

But not for long. I am a bit embarrassed to admit that while I occasionally miss my smaller bookstore, I have grown to love its oversized replacement. It has places to sit, tables where I can write, and even a cafe for a snack. I consider it my personal library. It is a great place to escape to a quieter mode. The catch? It can be a madhouse on weekends. On good days however, the unhurried, uncrowded floors lined with wonderful books become an inviting setting to which I can retreat.

And don't forget the public libraries. Libraries, especially the larger ones, are great places to spend an hour or more in relative solitude. Large tables, vast spaces, and dependable quiet all contribute to an ideal place to work, think, and imagine.

Follow the Plot

Cemeteries in the city tend to be overlooked as natural venues for solitude. When I lived in Toronto I remember spending a fair bit of time in the cemetery. Right in the middle of the city is a remarkable, upscale graveyard, notable for its plantings, walkways, and monuments. It was uncommonly quiet and surprisingly uplifting. And it was there that I did some of my best thinking and daydreaming.

Many of the larger cemeteries tend to be outside the city, yet many smaller, older ones are hidden behind churches or high walls. Better city maps will have them marked or if you have the patience and time to spare, call the city for information. Find out where your city's forefathers and foremothers were buried, and go visit.

Find a Moment Anywhere

We tend to think of finding solitude in quiet places and for longer periods of time. But small bits of time alone can also help relieve our stress. Our city lives are punctuated with such times. Opportunities when we can steal a brief moment or two for reflection or meditation. You can find morsels of quiet escape in the most unexpected places:

- waiting for that slow elevator to arrive
- waiting for a subway to come
- waiting for that cup of coffee to reheat
- waiting for that commercial to finish
- waiting for that light to change
- waiting in lines
- waiting for that secretary to take you off hold
- waiting in the doctor's or dentist's office
- sitting in traffic

Recognize and seize these valuable spare moments for yourself.

ESCAPING THE CITY

No city should be too large for a man to walk out of in a morning.

—CYRIL CONNOLLY

If we made two lists, one with all the reasons why we like living in the city and a second with all the reasons why we'd like to leave it, we would notice that many of the same items were on both lists. While we may relish the stimulation, the excitement, and the intensity of the city, there are times when we could do with a little less of it. Living in a big city is somewhat like eating too much rich food;

sometimes we crave salad. Sometimes we need to escape—at least for a while.

When I mentioned the phrase *escaping the city* to a friend, a big fan of the metropolis, he reacted with a touch of annoyance. "Too strong," he objected. "One escapes from prisons and jails. Living in the city hardly falls into that category." Maybe so. But there are times when a big city can overwhelm even the most urbane. Leaving the city, from time to time, becomes a necessary part of successful urban living. It provides balance and contrast. It allows you time to recharge and regroup before returning to the fray.

Get Away Often

The biggest mistake urban dwellers make is relying on their annual vacation to be an adequate time-out from the city. There is nothing wrong with a week in the Bahamas, a week in the mountains, or a trip to Disneyland. The problem is that these more traditional vacations tend to be the *only* time many city folk get out of town, and that is a mistake. If you live in a big city, these once-a-year getaways won't do it. By three p.m. on the Monday after you return, you find that you need another vacation. You also realize that the next major chunk of free time is fifty-one weeks away.

A better idea is to build in more frequent, shorter trips and vacations. These can take the form of half-days away, day trips, sleepovers, weekends, and long weekends. Think of time away as a safety valve that needs to be opened from time to time. The trick is to evenly distribute these getaways throughout your year, before the pressure builds.

Preschedule Time Away

The most common reason people give for not getting away is having too little time. They would love to get away, but something always comes up. I sympathize. I, too, know that the demands of life in the city are constant and unrelenting. But there is always something that will come up. If you decide to wait for that perfect time, you may end up never leaving the city.

Start by assuming that there will be no perfect time for you to get away but you are going to go anyway. Rather than reacting to an imposed schedule, create a vacation schedule early on that ensures that you will actually make it out of the city. Make time away from the city a priority in your life. Sit down with your calendar and block out some major time and a smattering of smaller time periods for venturing out of the city. Spread out the dates to cover various times of the year. Now you don't have to find the time—it's built in.

Build a Getaway File

If you are going to escape, you need to know where to escape to. It's amazing how little we know about getaway spots even a few hours from our city. Begin collecting places you can escape to. Start with the wonderful books on local travel at your bookstore. There are books describing all manners of trips, places to stay, and things to do and see. Include favorite places friends have told you about and articles from brochures, newspapers, and magazines. Have two categories: one for shorter trips lasting one or two days, and a second for longer trips. The kinds of places you might want to note for future reference could include:

- country inns
- bed-and-breakfasts
- health spas
- farms
- restaurants
- retreats
- tennis clubs
- ski resorts
- botanical gardens
- nature conservancies
- mansions and estates open to the public
- public gardens
- country auctions
- vineyards
- county fairs

Every little trip counts. Be creative and keep your eye out for opportunities, no matter how small.

Take a Day Trip

For an escape to be short, you have to be able to get there in an hour or less. The plan here is to get out of the city for a few hours or a full day and return the same day. Even without a car, you can make it out of town. Every city offers day excursions via public transportation to places and sites just outside of the city. You would be amazed at what there is to see and do in a day or less.

One of our favorite short trips out of the city is visiting a state park and forest about an hour away. In the middle of the park is a lake where you can rent canoes and small sailboats by the hour. We usually bring a picnic and have a small barbecue. It's a wonderful day away.

Take a Hike

Hiking in natural surroundings can have a soothing, calming effect on us. The views are often spectacular. Here, there are few elevators, virtually no fax machines, and barely a handful of beepers. And you have the chance to see other animals besides pigeons, mice, and roaches. For those who find wandering off into the wilderness a little intimidating, many routes allow you to park your car and follow a trail that will bring you back to your starting point. Organizations such as the Sierra Club are not only a good way of obtaining information about hikes, but they can also put you into contact with other people if you're short of company.

Bring Your Bike

While you certainly can bike in the city, finding a less congested road may have greater appeal. Once you get past the city boundary, there are many bicycle trails and open roads that offer great scenery and little traffic. A bicycle rack for your car is a terrific investment if you don't already have one.

Go to the Shore

A day at the shore can be a wonderful escape from the congestion and confusion of life in the city. Even if the water is too cold for swimming, strolling on a beach or a promenade above the water can be marvelously relaxing. Many forget about the shore during the off-season. That is a mistake. In the spring, fall, and winter months the beaches are beautiful and also wonderfully empty.

Just Pick

One of our other favorite outings as a family is to visit one of the many farms just outside the city. At different times of the year we are able to visit a farm and pick apples, blueberries, strawberries, or raspberries. Then we go home and figure out what to do with them. Pies are the simplest project, but we have recently ventured into the more arcane world of jams and jellies. Many of the farms offer other activities such as horseback riding and sampling the wonderful taste of fresh-pressed cider.

Freeload in the Suburbs

Think of it as a fair exchange. Suburbanites think nothing of using our cities to indulge themselves. They entertain themselves with our entertainment and gorge themselves at our restaurants. Why can't we avail ourselves of some of their amenities? I am sure you have at least one friend or family member who lives in the suburbs. We do, and when we are looking for a day outing we sometimes head out to the 'burbs. Our favorite destination is the community swimming pool, but there are other attractions. When the kids were small we would visit friends at Halloween and accompany them as they went door-to-door. The availability of tennis courts has not escaped our notice, either. And for a change of pace we take in a mall or two just to refresh our memories.

Stay in Country Inns

Small country inns and out-of-the-way bed-and-breakfasts provide the ideal contrast to the bustle and mass of the city. They are worlds away from the boring motels and hotels that dot the thruway. Meandering through country roads and byways, you can stay at that unique, one-of-a-kind hideaway that will not only provide you with a bed but also feed you home-cooked specialties.

Retreat for a While

There are times when you crave true quiet and a chance to be out of the city with nothing but your own thoughts. Fortunately, you can. Certain monasteries and convents welcome visitors into their midst. You would be surprised by the number of religious retreats that exist not too far from the city.

Swap Places

When the time comes for you to take a trip out of the city, remember that there are many who are more than willing to come into the city and would love to stay in a real home as opposed to the standard hotel room. Your home, for example. Yes, I know horror stories abound about people moving in and making a real mess of places. But I've heard more stories where things have worked out pretty well for everyone.

There are exchange agencies that can list your place in the city and provide you with listings of places in other areas around the world.

Time-Share

If you can't afford to own a place, it might be possible for you to time-share. This gives you part-time access to a place you might otherwise not be able to own. Some time-shares permit you to swap your designated times with others so that you can get away exactly when you want to.

Get Yourself Invited

People who do own a second home out of the city often get lonely. They need stimulation. You are the stimulation. You may already have friends and relations who regularly seek you out to join them in their nonurban sanctuaries. However, it may be the case that you are a few invites shy of your usual quota. Here are several field-tested lines that will bring even the most reticent country house-holders to their knees, begging for your company.

SUREFIRE INVITATION-GETTERS

Start with:

"What do you guys do when you have some vacation time?" (just to soften them up)

Proceed to:

"I'll bet your place in the country is simply marvelous! How lucky you are!"

"I'll bet the fall leaves (summer days, fresh snowfalls, spring flowers) are magnificent. Unfortunately, there were no seasons in my native country."

And the clincher:

"What I wouldn't give to spend even *one* day in a place like yours!"

If that doesn't snag you an invite, you are never going to see the inside of their medicine cabinet.

Find Your Own Second Home

A house out of town can be a wonderful antidote for the stress of the city. Just when you feel you are ready to go ballistic, you hop into your car and head for your personal retreat. "Yes," you reply, "that would be very nice, and so would having a villa on the Riviera where I could play backgammon and boules all day! Get real!"

I'm not talking waterfront, acreage, horses, or live-in help. I mean simple, very simple. There are many wonderful places you can find and not stay up all night wondering how you are going to pay for it.

Take a ride out into the country and begin looking around. Speak to the local Realtors and see what's on the market. If you are looking to buy cheap, avoid the trendy "in" places. You may find that you have to go a little farther out to save some money. Sharing a place with friends can work and save you lots. And if you find you are desperately unhappy, you can always sell it.

But Come Back

Hopefully, when you return, you will be refreshed, recharged, and happy to be back. Jump back in, embrace the city, and rejoice in all it has to offer. To paraphrase the words of Samuel Johnson: When you are tired of the big city, you are tired of life. And maybe, just maybe, he was right.